I Am a Troll

I Am a Troll

Inside the Secret World of the BJP's
Digital Army

Swati Chaturvedi

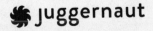

JUGGERNAUT BOOKS
KS House, 118 Shahpur Jat, New Delhi 110049, India

First published by Juggernaut Books 2016

ISBN 9789386228093

Typeset in Adobe Caslon Pro by R. Ajith Kumar, New Delhi

Printed at Replika Press Pvt. Ltd.

To my parents, Nisha and Gopal Chaturvedi,
with love and gratitude

Contents

Introduction

I am an investigative journalist. Freedom of expression is my bread and butter. Over the years I have had several cases filed against me by the Government of India (GOI), as have other Indian journalists, under the Official Secrets Act. I've proudly fought them all, as have the publications I worked with.

On 10 June 2015, I filed an FIR at south Delhi's Vasant Vihar police station against an anonymous Twitter handle, @lutyensinsider. @lutyensinsider had over 40,000 followers and had systematically targeted me over a period of six months in a vicious campaign that insinuated I had a sexual relationship with a politician.

Each day I would wake up to hundreds of notifications discussing my 'rate', 'last night's amazing anal sex' and the fictitious trysts where I 'the nymphomaniac could not get enough and was begging for more'. Yes, that was me being described on a public medium for posterity, my twenty-year-old professional career – which I take huge pride in – reduced to slander.

There was a base quality to these attacks, a hateful sexism that I had never encountered in all my years of being a reporter. My mornings were filled with rage and a sick, slightly nauseous feeling. The attacks were personal and after six months I had had enough.

My criminal complaint was the first of its kind filed by an Indian journalist under the sections of the Indian Penal Code that dealt with stalking, sexual harassment, transmitting obscene material over the Internet and outraging the modesty of a woman. Response was swift. Amid widespread media coverage, both national and international, Twitter suspended the handle for slander and harassment. It also gave the Delhi Police the IP address and email address of the anonymous slanderer. Unfortunately, there has been no arrest till date as the accused allegedly has powerful backers in the government.

@lutyensinsider hasn't been my only attacker. The threats of 'Nirbhaya-style' rape or 'an AK-

47 bullet' to get me to shut up about the pellet gun blindings in Kashmir after young militant Burhan Wani's death in July 2016 are my daily lot on Twitter. And I am not alone. Several other journalists, especially women, who have liberal political opinions and question government policies are routinely at the receiving end of violent, often sexually loaded, abuse from right-wing trolls.

Internet trolls are persons who sow discord on the Internet by starting arguments or upsetting people by posting inflammatory comments and images. They are the goons of the online world. In the case of India, online trolls usually have Hindu right-wing views and are highly nationalist. They tend to attack anyone who appears to be against the government, the Bharatiya Janata Party (BJP) or the nation. Some have a large number of followers. They usually have Hindu gods or the Twitter egg as their display pictures. Others have put up display pictures of beautiful women to increase their follower count. So you might see a user called 'Sonam' in a bikini tweeting hatred against Muslims. These trolls are mostly anonymous. Some, however, aren't and they are occasionally followed by high-profile members of the BJP, including Prime Minister Narendra Modi (see Chapter 1).

The latter tend to lead the charge, and as soon as they abuse you a swarm of anonymous trolls follow in their wake, either repeating the original abuse or adding to it. The anonymous swarm tweet extremely sexually explicit messages to women, sending images of pubic hair along with vulgar messages. The more famous the victims, the worse the abuse is. Well-known TV journalists like Barkha Dutt and Rajdeep Sardesai are among the most targeted by this group. Sometimes mobile numbers are shared on WhatsApp to get more feral trolls to join in the blood sport through another medium. Slurs such as 'sickular presstitute' are now par for the course.

Recently, playback singer Abhijeet, better known for leading a campaign to ban Pakistani singers from Bollywood, claimed on his verified Twitter account that the murder of Infosys techie Swathi in Chennai was an instance of 'love jihad'. Swathi had in fact been killed by a spurned admirer and a Hindu, who later committed suicide.

A verified Twitter handle is a much coveted

stamp given by Twitter to official government accounts, celebrities, world leaders and journalists. It essentially implies that your identity is not in doubt – you don't have a fake handle, you have been vetted by Twitter and you are an influencer within your world. Typically, Twitter verifies government issue identity documents as part of the process. It can also take away the blue verification tick in case of bad online behaviour.

The use of lies by verified Twitter users to generate communal hatred has always troubled me deeply. It's akin to giving them the equivalent of a megaphone and primetime TV slot. So I called out Abhijeet's lie and said it had the potential to cause riots. He retorted with a volley of abuses and unprintable expletives. This was followed by vicious trolling by a mob hiding behind anonymous Twitter handles. I filed another police case and Women and Child Development Minister Maneka Gandhi intervened to say she had decided to establish a special helpline: #IAmTrolledHelp.

But I'm not holding out for things to change. After all, no action has been taken against the Twitter users who shared fake images designed to fan communal passions after the September 2015 lynching of Mohammad Akhlaq in Dadri, Uttar Pradesh, for allegedly possessing beef.

In the United States, which is a beacon for free speech laws, thousands are arrested each year – and the courts uphold these allegations as 'actionable' – based on complaints from people who have received violent threats on social media. Hate speech, targeted harassment, threats of rape with graphic details of assault, incitement to violence – all this is 'actionable' too but our police does not act. Abhijeet openly issued a threat, 'main sabko dekh loonga [I will deal with everyone]', on national television in response to the story. The police did nothing other than registering a case.

My experiences, and those of my fellow citizens, have inspired this investigation. I had many questions and I wanted answers. Who are these trolls with their false names and fake photographs? Where do they come from? Why do they do what they do? Do they act as an organized whole or work spontaneously? Are they just fans of the BJP and Prime Minister Modi or is there a more formal link with the party?

The questions feel more urgent than ever. For one, the culture of online hate speech has spread to the real world. Union Minister of State for External Affairs and former army chief V.K. Singh used the phrase 'sickular presstitute' to describe leading journalists who have questioned him and the term has gone viral among BJP ministers and online right-wing trolls. After this, BJP Vice-President Dayashankar Singh called four-time Uttar Pradesh Chief Minister Mayawati 'worse than a prostitute'. Electoral exigencies and a collective howl of outrage from Parliament forced the party to suspend him for six years.

Words are never mere words. They can amplify actions, riots, violence. Take the case of the murder of Dr Pankaj Narang in Delhi on Holi in 2016. Rahul Raj (who tweets under the handle @bhak_sala and has 77,900 followers, including PM Modi) tweeted that the doctor was murdered by Muslims and that the media was hiding this information. Before any riots could break out, the Delhi Police had to issue a quick clarification that this was an outright lie. But they did not act against the handle for incitement or even register a case against the individual. I tracked the handle down. Its owner is a Bangalore-based manager who works at the multinational

Response to Rahul Raj's (bhak_sala) tweets on Dr Narang's murder

pharma company Novartis and runs a right-wing propaganda website called OpIndia. Novartis has not responded to my questions or to questions on social media by other users. Raj has also deleted the tweets. There are screenshots (*page 10*) of them taken from handles who retweeted his messages and criticized them at the time.

Earlier this year, BJP MP Hukum Singh claimed that an exodus of Hindus was taking place from Kairana in western Uttar Pradesh because they had been targeted by Muslims. Singh's claim was proved false but it nonetheless trended daily for two weeks until the National Human Rights Commission intervened. It's worth noting that subjects don't naturally trend on Twitter continuously for days and weeks. In the hotbed of Uttar Pradesh politics, especially before an election, such Chinese whispers can lead to lasting damage.

These are the things that inspired me to conduct such an extensive investigation. After PM Modi's government was sworn in nearly two and a half years ago, I've been watching in horrified fascination as the leader of the world's largest democracy follows and felicitates trolls. In the meantime, the online culture of right-wing harassment and attacks has grown steadily.

This investigation took me nearly two years and involved meeting actual trolls, BJP and RSS leaders, opposition leaders, and bureaucrats and officials working in government ministries. It has created a picture that leaves me extremely worried about our careless use of lies and hate online – and more importantly the ways in which some key ruling party leaders have used this as a political tool. For if you peddle lies and violence online, what does it say about your behaviour in the real world? I have never tracked such troubling faultlines in India's conversations with itself.

1

'Blessed to Be Followed by PM Modi'

Prime Minister Narendra Modi is very proud of his friendship with incumbent US President Barack Obama. Can you imagine Obama or Great Britain Prime Minister Theresa May, German Chancellor Angela Merkel or France President François Hollande following abusers on social media?

Mr Modi joined Twitter in 2009 and set up his personal website in February 2005. His party, the BJP, was the first Indian party to understand the power of social media and the Internet. They set up the party website in 1995 and were trained by the Rashtriya Swayamsevak Sangh (RSS), who went on to set up Internet shakhas in the early noughties (more on this unusual history later).

Contrast this with the Indian National Congress (INC), which set up its official website ten years later in 2005. Congress Vice-President

Rahul Gandhi only joined Twitter in 2015. The Aam Aadmi Party (AAP), which has a strong presence on social media, came into existence in November 2012. It had registered its website a couple of months earlier, in September.

Mr Modi has 21.6 million followers on Twitter and he follows 1375 people. In a Right to Information petition, the Prime Minister's Office (PMO) said that the PM's handles, @Narendramodi and @PMO, are run by the PM himself. Those who interact with him regularly (PMO officials, BJP leaders, etc.) allege he is obsessed with the platform and monitors social media carefully.

This leaves one enormously impressed at the amount of energy Mr Modi has but also leads to a darker question. Why does the PM of India alone among world leaders follow some of his country's worst online abusers? Among the handles followed by Modi, twenty-six accounts routinely sexually harass, make death threats and abuse politicians from other parties and journalists, with special attention given to women, minorities and Dalits. Describing themselves as 'proud Hindu', 'Garvit Hindu', 'desh bhakt', 'Namo

Bhakt', 'Bharat Mata Ki Jai' and 'Vande Mataram', these users are loud and proud, inevitably have a display picture with Mr Modi and proclaim to be 'blessed to be followed by the Prime Minister of India'.

When abused citizens tag Mr Modi and ask why he follows these handles, he maintains a resolute silence. There is no record of him, till this book went to press, of un-following even a single handle despite the registration of FIRs and in one case the suspension and return of a handle to Twitter.

Rather, the prime minister invited the people behind 150 of the handles he follows to a meet-and-greet called Digital Sampark on 1 July 2015 at his official residence, 7 Race Course Road (now called Lok Kalyan Marg). A number of the abusers quoted in this chapter tweeted pictures of themselves with the prime minister the next day and put them up as display pictures. This social media meet-and-greet was organized by the president of the BJP IT cell, Arvind Gupta, who chose the 'yodhas' (warriors), as they are officially described by the BJP and government ministers.

Meet PM Modi's trolls

Some of the handles in question are anonymous but most are not. There's Suresh Nakhua, who describes himself in his Twitter bio as

> vande mataram Hindu nationalist PM @NarendraModi follow me — blocked by India Today in Sep 14. Suspended by twitter for 24 hrs in Sep 14. Wholesale Trader (Pulses).

His profile has a picture of him shaking hands with Mr Modi, and he has also tweeted pictures of himself with Maharashtra Chief Minister Devendra Fadnavis. From the display pictures with PM Modi and Fadnavis, he looks like someone in his late forties, a portly man with curly black hair. He tweets messages such as:

> U asshole son of a bitch.... Did I abuse U? U confirmed tht u r product of a rape i.e. Balatkar ki paidaish

Suresh Nakhua's profile and his tweet to a Congress supporter, G. Surya

Mahaveer, @MahaveerM, is another notorious abuser, also 'Blessed 2 Be Followed by PM'. Like Nakhua, he too has been briefly suspended by Twitter for his vile words. Sample one of his tweets to Navendu Singh, an AAP supporter, on 16 August 2016:

Haha moron @NavenduSingh_ Don't fret. I can understand ur Mothers hole has become so Big, not worth opening too. Use sum lotion.

Screenshots of tweets by @MahaveerM, another notorious abuser

The right-wing trolls ran a campaign to overturn his Twitter suspension, 'I stand with Mahaveer', which was led by Giriraj Singh, Union Minister for Micro, Small and Medium Enterprises, who also follows him.

 **Giriraj Singh** ⊘
@girirajsinghbjp ⚙ +💼 Follow

I urge @TwitterIndia to reactivate @mahaveerm_ ...#IStandWithMahaveer

I request friends to RT to give strength to our voice ..

RETWEETS **938** FAVORITES **354**

BJP minister Giriraj Singh's tweets asking Twitter to overturn @MahaveerM's suspension

Twitter eventually complied. An unrepentant Mahaveer is still spreading bigotry. He tweeted recently:

citizen Ikhlaq killed by mob 45 lakh/4flats/ job!policemen Santosh killled by mob 20 lakhs! Money depends upon your religion

Mahaveer was tweeting about the lynching of Mohammad Akhlaq in Dadri in 2015 for allegedly eating beef – later it was found to be mutton – and claiming that his family was compensated far more than the family of the policeman killed in that riot. The handle had also tweeted explicit pictures of the slain policeman.

Author Shobhaa Dé tweeted condolences on BJP leader and minister Gopinath Munde's death on 3 June 2014, saying:

> shocking news about Munde's death. How tragic RIP. Burrey din aa gaye for family. Deepest condolences.

Harmless words on the demise of a popular leader, you would think, that too someone from the BJP. But Rahul Raj, @bhak_sala (see Introduction), had this to say:

> hi @DeShobhaa I understand your pain. Seems you did'int have sex for many days. Don't be so frustrated.

Mr Modi follows him and has done so for

years. Raj, as mentioned earlier, works at Novartis and runs the right-wing propaganda website OpIndia.

These are not just one-off tweets. Typically, such handles constantly peddle hate tweets and conspiracy theories and slander journalists, all of which form almost 90 per cent of their daily output.

Apart from attacking and sexually harassing journalists, most of these handles also continually tweet communal statements. Graphic pictures are posted of violence being inflicted by Muslims along with bloody images of cow slaughter – these are often taken from footage in Pakistan and Bangladesh and are passed off as Indian with the audio suppressed.

On occasion, high-profile right-wing sympathizers also join the chorus. One such offender is academic and activist Madhu Kishwar, who has more than 576,000 followers, including PM Modi. When challenged by various journalists and social media users for falsely passing off a Pakistani video as Indian, she simply said she had received it on WhatsApp and didn't remove it. But in most cases when the veracity of a picture or a video is challenged, it is pulled down immediately.

Such posts are designed to stir up trouble and are often accompanied with what appears to be a coordinated hashtag campaign where a countless number of anonymous Twitter handles retweet the same tweet continuously until the subject starts trending. An example of this is #whataboutMalda, which refers to an attack by Muslims on a police station in the Bengal district and alludes to a media cover-up of it during the West Bengal state elections in 2016.

'Satyasadhak truth seeker' @RituRathaur, who is a BJP worker with 594,000 followers, tweeted an inflammatory picture of an Uttar Pradesh policeman who was allegedly run over by cow smugglers after Mohammad Akhlaq was attacked. Several journalists alerted Uttar Pradesh Chief Minister Akhilesh Yadav, who promptly got the state police to register an FIR against her for communal incitement. The state government also immediately clarified on Twitter that the picture was false and that the policeman had been killed 'while trying to stop truck of river stones'.

Arvind Gupta denied to me that Ritu Rathaur had anything to do with the BJP social

Arvind Gupta @buzzindelhi 59m
Support our SM volunteers when they
have done no wrong and are being
politically targeted
#IstandWithRituRathaur

↩   ♻ 320   ★ 117   +👤

Arvind Gupta @buzzindelhi 8h
@bainjal You are making a baseless
statement. @Riturathaur is not part of
BJP IT/SM team @nesoron
@Rohinisgh @Joydas @UPGovt
@yadavakhilesh

↩   ♻ 60   ★ 26   +👤

BJP social media cell chief Arvind Gupta's tweets in support of
@RituRathaur

media team. Yet within hours, he was tweeting
#IstandWithRituRathaur, a hashtag started by
right-wing supporters to put pressure on the
Uttar Pradesh government and Twitter not to
act against her and referring to her as one of
'our SM [social media] volunteers'. His tweet
was immediately retweeted 320 times. Rathaur
regularly tweets videos of gory cow slaughter and
imaginary instances of love jihad, including the
Tuktuki Mondal incident in Bengal, as a cursory
glance at her timeline will reveal.

In many instances, online bad behaviour spills over into real life – and in unexpected ways.

On 7 September 2016, Tinu Jain, the founder of the Narendra Modi Army Brigade, who is followed by PM Modi on Twitter and has the obligatory display picture with him, was arrested for running a sex racket in Gwalior, Madhya Pradesh. The police arrested him from a spa in what they described as a 'compromising position'. AAP wasted no time in starting the hashtag #NamoSexArmy, which trended for several hours. Ironically, this bhakt had last tweeted 'in whatever way I am standing in front of you I have nothing to hide'.

Then there's Priti Gandhi, who tweets at @MrsGandhi and has three pictures with Mr Modi on her profile. She has also tweeted that she's 'a huge fan of Nathuram Godse' and mocks women who face sexual abuse and harassment, calling them 'attention seekers who should get out of the kitchen if they can't stand the fire'. Gandhi was thrown out of the BJP when she tweeted a fake endorsement of Mr Modi by Julian Assange of WikiLeaks before the 2014 general election. This was denied by Assange and caused the BJP considerable embarrassment. Meenakshi Lekhi, BJP leader and currently MP, went on national television and disowned Gandhi, saying the BJP had nothing to do with her regarding the matter. But she was quietly taken back by the party after the furore died down. She is now a national executive member of the BJP Mahila Morcha, the women's wing of the party.

Online abuse sometimes leads to actual violence. Tajinder Pal Singh Bagga, @TajinderBagga, describes himself as a 'Swayamsevak, editor @ theNaMoPatrika, convenor @BSKS_India [Bhagat Singh Kranti Sena] and @ModiFyingIndia, ex-National Executive Member, BJP youth'. In October 2011, he barged into lawyer and activist Prashant Bhushan's chambers with another person and attacked him. Bhushan has publicly supported a referendum in Kashmir to determine if the local population wants the army to maintain internal security. An FIR was filed against Bagga, but it was never followed up.

On occasion, Modi's online army even attacks his own party members. Meenakshi Lekhi was hounded on Twitter by avowed BJP supporters because she shared a stage with Barkha Dutt in her constituency. A harried Lekhi then publicly called out some of the handles followed by Modi as 'idiots' and 'lobbyists'.

When Maneka Gandhi, as Minister for Women and Child Development, tried to put a stop to the incessant cyber bullying and violence against women by setting up a helpline called #IAmTrolledHelp, the right-wing trolls went ballistic. Even handles being followed by PM Modi trolled her. Gandhi was accused of trying to stop freedom of expression and was forced to hastily clarify that she was only going to look at complaints, not monitor social media.

In an interview to Aaj Tak four days after my run-in with Abhijeet, Gandhi said she was setting up the helpline because 'that singer's tweets were absolutely unacceptable'. She also called a meeting with Twitter officials. Till date, her ministry is following up some complaints, with zero results I might add.

This episode had a hilarious side effect as some trolls publicly outed themselves. For instance, @rishibagree – followed by Mr Modi – made a plaintive appeal to BJP President Amit Shah, tweeting:

We spend 6 to 8 hours on social media for BJP spoiling our health not giving time to our families only to be attacked by Maneka.

Another anonymous handle tagged the prime minister and tweeted:

This is an attack on your online support base.

But why should any leader or party crave a support base which makes violent threats against women, issues death threats and spreads communal canards?

Some more posts by Modi's trolls

(Left) *A Twitter troll being felicitated by Prime Minister Modi* and (right) *examples of abusive tweets*

29

Sexist photoshopped picture of former actress Gul Panag tweeted by a BJP handle when she joined the Aam Aadmi Party

'Blessed to Be Followed by PM Modi'

Abusive tweets by Bharat_Mata_Ki_Jay, also 'humbled' to be followed by Prime Minister Modi

A Twitter handle which is followed by Prime Minister Modi abusing senior journalist Barkha Dutt

Rahul Roushan, who has a verified blue tick from Twitter, also includes PM Modi among his followers. He is the chief strategy officer of Swarajya, a media group which also brings out OpIndia.

On 31 October 2016, the Madhya Pradesh police killed eight undertrials in an 'encounter', an extra-judicial killing. Video and audio have emerged proving that the men were shot dead in cold blood.

Here is Roushan the journalist asking for the 'executions' of undertrials without due process and also saying that the state should not bother to arrest suspects but 'kill in cold blood'. The tweet asking for 'cold blooded' murder was retweeted over a thousand times. He has 56,200 followers.

Roushan, according to his Twitter bio, is based in Mumbai. He also abused another handle by tweeting: 'Obviously I endorse cold blooded murder of terrorists.' The eight undertrials who were 'encountered' were not convicted of any crime and two were on the verge of being released.

For a list of the top trolls followed by PM Modi, refer to Appendix A.

'Blessed to Be Followed by PM Modi'

Tweets by verified Twitter user Rahul Roushan, the chief strategy officer of the media group Swarajya

The trickle-down effect

The trickle-down effect of PM Modi following abusers on Twitter is apparent in the coarse discourse used by his ministers. And it's not just V.K. Singh and Dayashankar Singh.

Giriraj Singh is always asking journalists to 'go to Pakistan' and has repeatedly asked anyone who disagrees with BJP to apply 'Burnol', referring to the popular burn cream. Abhisar Sharma of ABP News has been regularly attacked by Singh, as have other journalists and writers who took part in 'award wapsi' and were asked to go to Pakistan.

BJP's Anil Vij is the Haryana sports minister who led a large junket to the 2016 Rio Olympic Games. Tweeting from a verified Twitter handle, he posted on 2 September: 'Some stinking dogs are writing again and again that we forgot to buy tickets for Rio which is incorrect.' Not only was Vij playing to the gallery of trolls by abusing journalists but the tweet was also promoted, i.e., paid to be advertised within Twitter.

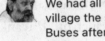

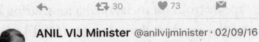

Haryana Sports Minister Anil Vij refers to journalists as 'stinking dogs'

Former human resource development minister Smriti Irani was, until recently, known for her daily Twitter spats. Her Twitter battle with Bihar Education Minister Dr Ashok Choudhary, who addressed her as 'Dear Smriti ji', left people stunned. It all started when Choudhary made a query about education funds for Bihar and used the innocuous 'dear' as a suffix. Irani took exception to the term and asked how he could dare to address her so.

Irani has called Barkha Dutt a 'liar' during the JNU student leader crisis, much to the orgiastic delight of trolls, and has regularly attacked journalists rudely. The most extreme episode was when a minor Congress spokesperson, Priyanka Chaturvedi, was threatened with a 'Nirbhaya-style' rape by trolls on social media for sharing her views on the goods and services tax (GST) which the BJP was trying to introduce in Parliament. Irani, tone deaf to another woman's plight, wanted to know why Chaturvedi was worried about her security and proclaimed in an interview to NDTV that by attacking Chaturvedi, Irani had given a new lease of life to her faltering career.

What has never been clear is how organized

this trolling is, or if the trolls are officially linked to the party or are simply a horde of unruly and enthusiastic fans. In the following chapters, a few trolls and an ex-member of the BJP's social media cell provide for the first time eyewitness accounts to the workings of the party's digital wing.

Officially, however, PM Modi has always kept silent on this issue. Senior BJP leader and Finance Minister Arun Jaitley has said that while he personally does not approve of the horrific trolling that BJP supporters indulge in, there is nothing that the government can do about it. Many party leaders take such a line to distance themselves from the online viciousness. Yet what's clear is that some office-bearers of the party – Arvind Gupta, Giriraj Singh and Priti Gandhi – have publicly supported these trolls, while the PM himself continues to follow some of the offenders.

It's also worth noting that three members of PM Modi's cabinet have put social media to innovative and effective real-time use. External Affairs Minister Sushma Swaraj responds to Indians in trouble all over the world on a range of issues such as passports and lost documents and replies to stranded citizens in conflict zones. She has carved out a new image and constituency for herself. Her wit and humour were evident when she told a user that she was too busy aiding Indians in distress to help him with his complaint about a refrigerator. Swaraj's Twitter persona has won her praise even from the BJP's critics. Suresh Prabhu and Maneka Gandhi too have used Twitter to help citizens with their efforts to provide real-time aid in railway services and the establishment of the #IAmTrolledHelp helpline respectively.

The global culture of vicious online hate speech which has permeated every sphere must be acknowledged. India's troll culture can be placed within this context. Members of AAP also do their share of trash talk by regularly making topics like 'Modi And Madhuri' and 'Modi's snoopgate' trend, though they stop short at issuing death and rape threats and sharing inflammatory videos and images.

Ankit Lal, head of IT and innovation for AAP, told me they did not have a paid social media army but only volunteers, and did not believe in using sexual harassment as a weapon against women journalists. Yet AAP quickly gets nasty with journalists who criticize the party or their leader, Arvind Kejriwal. Witness a recent example when Kejriwal himself attacked former editor of the *Indian Express* Shekhar Gupta by calling him a 'dalal' (broker) of the Congress and now a 'dalal' of Modi, bringing disrepute to journalism because Gupta had called out a malaria death in Delhi.

Yet there's no question that right-wing representatives dominate India's online political discourse and show more ugliness and violence than anyone else. The language used by associated ministers and officials is profoundly troubling too, apart from being wholly inappropriate. More worrying are the political consequences when the loose talk of party supporters and official-speak merge.

Take the open gloating on Twitter at the pellet blindings in Kashmir during the protests that followed Burhan Wani's death. This was accompanied by calls on social media for the mass murder of Kashmiris. One handle called @ggiittiikkaa with 80,000 followers – including Prime Minister Modi – tweeted pictures of Wani's funeral procession and added

20K attended funeral of terrorist Burhan. Should have dropped a bomb and given permanent Azadi to these 20K pigs.

 गीतिका
@ggiittiikkaa

🔲 Follow

20K attended funeral of terrorist Burhan. Should have dropped a bomb and given permanent Azadi to these 20K pigs 😢

RETWEETS LIKES
1,091   1,018

9:24 AM - 9 Jul 2016

Tweet following the funeral of Burhan Wani calling for the mass murder of twenty thousand Kashmiris

This call for the mass murder of Kashmiris was retweeted 1184 times and liked 1086 times.

'BJP is in a coalition government in Jammu & Kashmir. Should the PM really follow handles that want mass murder to be carried out against citizens for attending a funeral in India's most sensitive state?' asks ABP News editor Abhisar Sharma, who claims he has been a victim of organized trolling by right-wing users.

Sharma, who has virtually stopped tweeting after the intense harassment of himself and his family, says, 'It seems to me that the social media wing of the ruling dispensation is involved in trolling and abusing liberals who dare to ask uncomfortable questions of the Modi government. I believe it's organized. When I see ministers like Giriraj Singh defending and appealing for asking the reinstatement of abusive handles, what other conclusion can I come to?

'The silence of the PM on these issues has now resulted in shocking attacks on Dalits and Muslims. The monster seems to have slipped out of their control. It gives an ideal atmosphere for forces across the border for their propaganda to feed on the insecurity of the minorities. Is this what we really want?'

For example, the tweet calling for the mass murder of Kashmiris went viral in Pakistan and contributed greatly towards intensifying anti-India feelings in the country, Sharma points out.

The anguished cry from Kashmiri IAS topper Shah Faesal about the 'studios reflecting the street' and creating false binaries shows how polarized the discourse has become. After Faesal's distressing piece on Facebook in July 2016 was reproduced in the *Indian Express* he was predictably attacked as a 'traitor' and 'terrorist' by party loyalists like Ashoke Pandit, who was appointed to the Central Board of Film Certification by the Modi government.

As an IAS official bound by service conduct rules, Faesal has no right to reply unless he gets clearance from the Government of India. The same month, the government changed the Department of Personnel and Training rules. It had always stated that no official could write anything without taking permission from the government. Now this was extended to social media.

In an interview to me, Arun Shourie, former BJP minister, ex-party member and fierce critic of Modi, summarizes some of these concerns eloquently. 'By following them Modi is giving the message: I am following it. [If] You are following, then you are encouraging it. Next I hear he had a reception for them. You are receiving the same fellows in the PM's official residence. Then the encouraged fellows put up their photos with Modi. Next I heard one of them had been made the chief of the BJP's IT cell, so obviously it's now a party operation, one of the many operations being used to silence voices in the whole country.'

2

The BJP Connection

How close is the connection of the vast troll army with the BJP? Are they paid? Are they organized? The BJP has a social media cell in its 11 Ashoka Road office. Its official duty is to highlight PM Modi's and the party's achievements and to make them trend, but the cell's boss, Arvind Gupta, personally supports some of the trolls on Twitter. I met over thirty BJP social media volunteers who painted a similar picture of their work (see Chapter 3) on conditions of anonymity. Then I met Sadhavi Khosla, a former BJP social media cell member, who came forward to tell her story. But before we get to that, here is some background.

The 2014 elections

In Lance Price's book *The Modi Effect*, Arvind Gupta, who has been working with the BJP since

2010, says that 'the Modi camp felt "powerless" about getting heard in mainstream media. Our response was totally dependent on them and what they decided to report'. According to Gupta, 'social media changed the entire scenario' – and it was the RSS that provided the crucial training (see Chapter 5), pointing to its deep organizational understanding of social media and its powers. Price also wrote that 'from his early days as CM [chief minister] in Gujarat, Modi has been convinced that the media, especially the English media, is out to undermine him at any and every opportunity. For Modi social media is not just a passion, but a necessity.'

Social media was thus a central factor in Modi's win in the 2014 election. The BJP social media cell's outreach, under the management of Arvind Gupta, is widely regarded as one of the most effective political campaigns the country has seen. But even during the elections, the behaviour of its members and the possibilities of what you could or could not do online raised troubling questions.

Former chief election commissioner S.Y. Quraishi, whose responsibility it was to ensure fair and regulated elections, had wanted the Election Commission's (EC) guidelines for the media for politicians and political parties during elections to be extended to social media as well.

He argues that the funding limit for candidates and political parties should hold true for social media too. He believes even the content used by political parties in advertisements ought to be cleared by the EC to ensure that no sections of the Indian Penal Code, including communal incitement and Section 150 (hiring, or conniving at hiring, of persons to join unlawful assembly), are violated.

All political parties by law have to declare their media spend to the EC. But you can spend as much as you like on digital media and come under no scrutiny during an election campaign with no questions raised about content either. This explains the increasing focus on social media as the new battleground.

With real-time campaigns being carried out on social media the EC, according to Dr Quraishi, is incapable of monitoring hate content or incitement. Anonymity on Twitter gives a further fillip to such incendiary content, giving political parties the shield of deniability.

Dr Quraishi says ruefully, 'This can be overcome quite easily once deterrent action is taken. The police is empowered to act on the EC's directions during elections. But in the case of hate mongering and communal incitement sponsored by an influential political party, the police often register a case, but simply choose not to act, giving immunity and encouragement to paid trolls.'

This perhaps explains the burgeoning growth of the social media cells of major political parties, with their unlimited and unaccounted spending. I ask Dr Quraishi about the fate of his proposal. He smiles and says there was huge resistance with some saying it was an attack 'on freedom of expression and charges of trying to police social media'. This was neither the intent nor the plan. It would not have affected the common man, only political parties who would have to declare how much they were spending on social media and what the contents of their advertisements were.

Recall the infamous cow advertisement issued by the BJP just before the 2015 assembly elections in Bihar. It was openly inflammatory and led to the EC cracking the whip and asking for the ad to be withdrawn. While the BJP was forced to pull out the offensive advertisement from print and electronic media, it had already hit social media and was circulated widely.

The cell on Ashoka Road

Today, two years after the elections, Gupta and his team have moved from running the election campaign to running the party's social media cell. Controlled by Gupta, it operates out of the BJP's headquarters at 11 Ashoka Road in New Delhi. The cell is made up of key members who ensure that certain hashtags, decided by Gupta, are made to trend on social media on a particular day.

They also send out instructions to a large network of social media workers across India – this is partly made up of party volunteers who are assigned to the IT cell and partly paid workers – about the tweet agenda for the day. A lot of it is standard PR – tweeting routine addresses by PM Modi and Amit Shah or creating BJP-

or Mr Modi-related trend topics. So you will see thousands of identically worded tweets on 'VishvaGuruPM' praising the PM or trending in support of one of their own.

The BJP had with foresight created a bank of thousands of dormant Twitter accounts when the verification process was less stringent. These are accounts of party workers to be used when needed. The BJP uses them for their storms of synchronized tweeting. They also have bots controlled by the party's central IT cell which tweet out identical messages simultaneously. These are algorithms acting in social media networks which to the outside world look like a real user. The cell thus essentially works through repetition and the flooding of timelines with a particular tweet. It is given a line which is then tweeted out from multiple Twitter accounts within seconds. The same is the case with trending hashtags.

The BJP social media cell is a superbly organized centre which is highly effective in spreading messages. What has never been clear is the exact relationship it has with the online right-wing trolls and to what extent the daily coordination extends to them as well. My conversations with a number of social media workers and Sadhavi Khosla proves that there is a clear link between the two and that 11 Ashoka Road controls much of the online trolling.

Khosla's story

For the young entrepreneur Sadhavi Khosla 5 December 2013 was a very special day. Khosla runs a knowledge process outsourcing (KPO) company in what is now Gurugram. She got a call from then Gujarat chief minister Narendra Modi's office telling her that the CM appreciated her work on social media. She was extended a personal invitation to join the BJP's social media team.

Khosla had been tweeting about the need for change, how endemic corruption was destroying India and how a strong leader was the need of the hour. After the call, Mr Modi also started following her on Twitter, which he continues to do till date.

Khosla is an attractive thirty-seven-year-old management professional from Panjab University. She has a specialization in marketing and spent six years in the US before returning to India to

Khosla in her BJP social media cell T-shirt

be with her parents and bring up her son in her home country. She was ecstatic at the phone call. Her idol, the man she wanted to see as the PM of India, had asked her to join a movement to change India, to bring in development and herald 'achhe din'.

Khosla put everything aside and joined the social media cell as an unpaid volunteer, throwing herself into campaigning for Modi 24/7. She was part of the famous 'chai pe charcha' plan and organized many of them in Gurugram. So what turned the young woman from a fervent supporter and believer of Mr Modi to someone terrified of the BJP's social media cell?

As she told me her story over several sessions, she dissolved into tears time and time again. It was unsettling to watch this beautifully dressed, vivid, confident woman break down repeatedly. So much so that I had to once take her out of a public place where people were beginning to stare. '*Main prayischit karna chahati hoon* [I want to atone for the sin that I have committed],' she told me emotionally.

This is why she decided to come out.

Khosla comes from a family that has for three generations supported the Congress. Her grandfather Surender Nath Khosla was a freedom fighter and a Congress MLA from Samana in Punjab. But she had moved towards the BJP in the run-up to the 2014 election, 'convinced that the country would finally develop and the corruption and inertia that characterized United Progressive Alliance [UPA] rule would change only if Mr Modi became PM'.

The young woman is deeply religious – she can recite the Bhagavad Gita and the Ramayana – and the indoctrination was facilitated by her piety. It began when she moved to Michigan in 2004 with her engineer husband, who was then working for Hewlett Packard. Khosla was employed at a health care company. Soon, she and a group of Indians, all highly paid professionals, started receiving anonymous chain mails. The mails, some of which ran into a hundred pages, made startling claims against the Congress. They said that Sonia Gandhi had conspired against Rajiv Gandhi as part of her anti-Hindu stance, that Priyanka Gandhi was bipolar and had separated from her husband Robert Vadra, that Rahul Gandhi was a drug addict and married to a non-Hindu and had children but this was kept hidden. Over the years they also had reams on the corrupt deals of P. Chidambaram and on Barkha Dutt, her Nira Radia connection and her 'Muslim husbands'.

Khosla says this content was identical to the WhatsApp forwards she saw later – once she joined the BJP social media team – which were directed to be tweeted by Gupta and his team. She still has some of those chain letters and says, 'We were ordered to repeatedly tweet these slanderous claims by Gupta. Slowly, along with the Anna Hazare movement, these became the accepted narrative about the Gandhi family because even they never rebutted the allegations. I have done my MBA in marketing yet I was completely taken in by these claims. I believed them fervently as the truth.'

Once Khosla was on board she was asked to meet and have the customary chat with Arvind Gupta, who headed the National Digital Operations Centre (NDOC), the official name for the social media cell which was leading volunteers for Mission 272+, the digital campaign for the 2014 election. 'I was ushered into this huge room where Gupta, a very ordinary-looking man, was completely dwarfed by multiple giant 56-inch TV screens, which were crunching real-time data of social media trends and ensuring certain hashtags trended.'

Recalling her first encounter with Gupta, Khosla's ever present smile disappears. 'He seemed to be extremely preoccupied. I was told the goal was to attack and expose the UPA government and the Gandhi family. He said that he and his team of social media in-charges used to have a teleconference with Modi ji every night. If Modi ji was busy in the campaign the conference call would happen even past midnight. Modi ji was personally monitoring all social media activity regarding the campaign. All of us social media volunteers knew that Arvind Gupta was in daily touch with Modi ji and because of this he had huge power and an aura.'

During the 2014 election, Gupta ran the biggest ever social media operation in the country. He had a team of around 200 people in Delhi alone; some paid and the others volunteers whose travel, food and living expenses were taken care of by the BJP. Some like Khosla accepted no payment and took near-sabbaticals from their work. The paid techies came to Ashoka Road daily as part of their 9-to-5 routine and worked fulltime. There was also a door-to-door campaign for increasing the volunteer base, with BJP social media workers going from building to building in Gurugram recruiting people for the cell from a database they had collected. This was replicated on a bigger scale in Ahmedabad and Vadodara in Gujarat with nearly 2000 people on the rolls.

These volunteers and employees were given a 'hit list' of mainstream journalists who needed to be constantly attacked. This included NDTV's Barkha Dutt and Rajdeep Sardesai, who was with CNN-IBN at the time. 'If there was even an unfavourable mention of Modi ji anywhere, Gupta's digital tracking tools would pick it up and the pack of hyena-like trolls would descend.'

In her unbounded enthusiasm Khosla gave up all her work and her social life to focus on Mission 272+. 'You know I didn't go out for dinner for a year,' she says, laughing. Khosla's KPO, which she had set up two years previously, was doing brisk business because of her network of contacts in the US. 'I used to travel to the US every two months to ensure that I met my clients and kept them happy. My business took a huge hit because of my passionate devotion to the Modi campaign. I lost two big contracts as I stopped travelling. But I was so thoroughly engrossed in the campaign that even this did not bother me.'

Her points of contact were two BJP members, Vishal Gupta and Nitin Kashyap, both of whom still work for Gupta. They used to manage WhatsApp. Volunteers like Khosla would be sent

WhatsApp messages about what to tweet and target for trends each day. It was a never-ending stream. 'Gupta would get angry if they were not put out verbatim,' says Khosla.

The NDOC had a single-point brief to all WhatsApp groups – troll the Gandhis and mock them. 'All the propaganda and cartoons created against the Gandhi family were done in the NDOC and the volunteers were asked to make them trend and flood social media. Yaar, even the jokes on Robert Vadra and Rahul Gandhi were created in the NDOC and we were told to use them to create a flood.' Apart from this, volunteers like Khosla also helped with the individual campaigns of some candidates.

A core cell of approximately fifty worked with Gupta in the headquarters and followed his direct instructions. They managed a host of volunteers like Khosla, who would receive daily messages. There were twenty or twenty-one WhatsApp groups, which were further subdivided into categories such as professionals and women's groups. On special occasions, Gupta would send out instructions directly to the whole base.

'Gupta had the final authority. Once he sent out a WhatsApp message it was to be followed without question. You could not challenge it since he derived his authority from Modi.'

The first shock came when Khosla and her group were treated rudely by Smriti Irani. She and her band of social media volunteers had organized a programme in a park in Gurugram. Irani arrived on time and berated the organizers in front of a huge media contingent for the small turnout. Then she started abusing the media that was present. Khosla says, 'I was shocked. It had rained and the crowd was very small. But she just got so aggressive and attacked the media and told them not to cover the event while telling us that such a small crowd was an insult to her. I was asked later by BJP Mission 272+ to go and work for her campaign in Amethi. I refused and instead worked with Kirron Kher and campaigned for her in Chandigarh.'

Khosla was still caught up in her enthusiasm for the development model promised by Mr Modi and these small hiccups did not cause any disenchantment. She was idealistic enough to believe that she had a role to play in 'transforming India – throwing out a corrupt regime and finally giving Hindus their due'.

Mr Modi won the election and the social media cell, whose brief had been to ensure victory, continued to function in war mode. After the win, the cell, Khosla claims, 'actually got bigger since they now have huge funding and new enemies are found every day to attack and target. With the UP elections coming up [in early 2017] the BJP's social media cell is expanding.'

The flood of bile Khosla was expected to promote slowly started getting to her. 'It was a never-ending drip feed of hate and bigotry against minorities, the Gandhi family, the journalists on the hit list, liberals…anyone perceived as anti-Modi.' As the months went by, she felt that the development agenda she had voted for was put on the backburner while the culture of hate seemed to be growing larger. This was not why she had joined.

Khosla tweeted about the drug epidemic in Punjab at least 5000 times over 2014 and 2016 and also tagged PM Modi. She had lost a close friend to the addiction and was very active against the state's drug menace. Mr Modi refused to respond.

*Khosla at her home with the BJP social media women's group
during a Chai Pe Charcha meet organized by her* (above) *and
with Kirron Kher* (below)

'Here was the PM who I thought would sweep out corruption not saying a word about Punjab because the BJP was in alliance with the Akali Dal, the ruling party in the state. I was very hurt. The same Modi responds to the abusive trolls he follows and even sends them birthday greetings. I genuinely believed in him and worked 24/7 to bring him into power yet he did not even acknowledge my legitimate concern. That was quite painful.'

The abuse and trolling now began to frighten and upset her. 'I simply could not follow Gupta's directions any more when I saw rape threats being made against female journalists like Barkha Dutt, who had been my idol when I was a kid. I had even copied her hairstyle in school. And here we were supposed to attack her in filthy terms. Every day some new person was a target and they would attack like a swarm of bees with vile sexual innuendoes, slander, rape and death threats. It made me feel sick and suffocated as a woman. I had not signed up for this.'

Khosla refused to tweet the Barkha abuse but she didn't always have a choice. On Gupta's instructions, Khosla trolled Rajdeep Sardesai about his '50 crore bungalow' and was blocked by him. She also trolled Robert Vadra on his DLF deals and Rahul Gandhi on his sabbatical. 'You had to do it if [the instructions] came from Gupta. Most volunteers in the social media cell sent out identical tweets. I never tweeted abuse or rape and death threats to anyone,' says Khosla, an expression of guilt and grief on her face. 'These are my regrets, that I believed their lies, and this is what I want to atone. I later messaged Sardesai when he quit Twitter asking him to come back and he was incredibly nice and even unblocked me.'

Khosla had even raised her concerns with the pioneer of social media in the RSS and the BJP, Ram Madhav (see Chapter 5), who she says 'frightened me less than Gupta', in a Google Hangout earlier in 2014 where she was selected to participate by the social media cell. 'I asked him directly about the huge lack of respect the RSS seems to have for women, which he denied. Ram Madhav ji heard me out very patiently and said, "You have a very apt name for our party, Sadhavi, it goes very well with the BJP. Focus on the positives. These things should be ignored."'

In the meantime, her work was beginning to

affect her home life. Her father, a retired Class I officer in the Punjab government, a staunch Congress supporter, stopped talking to her because he felt she was doing something wrong. 'For the two years I was in the BJP, he refused to say a single word to me. That hurt so much. Even my mother used to mock me, saying, "Where is your achhe din, beta? They have made a fool out of you."'

At the dinner table, Khosla would often find herself saying something anti-Muslim, coloured by the voices that surrounded her during the day. Khosla's husband reminded her one day, 'Do you remember that the first nanny we had for our son in the US was Pakistani? How lovingly she cared for him. Would you even employ her now as you seem to be getting so bigoted?' Her husband's gentle inquiry pierced the 'brainwashed bubble I was inhabiting'. Sobbing, she says, 'My son is dearer to me than my life and his first nanny was a Pakistani and here I was turning into a bigot.' The incident was to be a turning point for her.

By end 2015, two years after she had joined, Khosla's disenchantment was complete.

The breaking point was the attacks on the two

ruling Khans of Bollywood – Aamir and Shah Rukh. Shah Rukh Khan had talked about his fears of the intolerance growing in India in an interview with NDTV in November 2015. His comments created a controversy and there was an online campaign to boycott his film *Dilwale* before its release in December 2015. The star was forced to apologize for his statements.

Three weeks later, at an event organized by the *Indian Express*, Aamir Khan had spoken about his 'sense of insecurity' because of the increasing intolerance and mentioned his wife Kiran Rao's fears about bringing up their child in India.

Khan was abused in the worst possible way with trolls asking him and his wife to join the Islamic State terrorist group if he wanted to feel safe. The Ministry of Tourism immediately dropped him as the brand ambassador of their Incredible India campaign. Arvind Gupta also messaged all the party's social media volunteers directing them to endorse a petition addressed to Snapdeal asking for Khan to be dropped from their advertisements. After facing the wrath of BJP supporters, who downgraded the Snapdeal app on Google Play and the iOS App Store on orders from Gupta,

Snapdeal terminated its contract with Khan and issued the following statement:

> Snapdeal is neither connected nor plays a role in comments made by Aamir Khan in his personal capacity. Snapdeal is a proud Indian company built by passionate, young Indians focused on building inclusive India. Every day we are positively impacting thousands of small businesses and millions of consumers in India. We will continue our mission of creating one million successful online entrepreneurs in India.

'The campaign against Aamir was the last nail in the coffin for my association with the BJP and forced me to part ways with a party and PM I had passionately supported. The poisonous campaign launched by the BJP's social media team proved Aamir's point on intolerance.'

Khosla believes that the decision to go after Khan had the blessings of PM Modi and BJP President Amit Shah. She says, 'When nothing in the BJP or the government moves without their approval, there was no way Arvind Gupta could have decided to go after an actor using the party's entire social media team without a go-ahead from the duo.'

Gupta kept quiet on the attack he had organized but Defence Minister Manohar Parrikar referred to it and inadvertently hinted at the role of the BJP social media cell in a speech in July 2016. Speaking at a book launch he said, 'People have shown their power; an actor made this mistake, said his wife wants to go and stay in a foreign country. That was an arrogant statement.' He added, 'Some of our people are very smart, I know. There was a team working on this. They were telling people you order and return. The company should learn a lesson; they had to pull his advertisement.'

The statements were clearly aimed at Aamir Khan, although Parrikar did not name the actor or Snapdeal. Khosla in response tweeted:

Parrikar was right when he said @aamir_khan was taught a lesson as I recvd this whatsapp from BJP social media head.

She then reached out to me.

'I had always looked at Shah Rukh as "Raj" and "Rahul", Salman as "Prem" and Aamir for

Instruction from Arvind Gupta to Khosla on WhatsApp regarding the Snapdeal petition

his acting and suddenly for the first time in twenty-five years they simply became Muslims to be targeted and trolled,' she says. 'Both Gupta's decisions and WhatsApp messages to attack Shah Rukh and Aamir really bothered me and I couldn't

Sign the Petition to Snapdeal India · Appeal Snapdeal to drop Aamir Khan from their ads · Causes - https://www.causes.com/actions/1782347-sign-the-petition-to-snapdeal-india?utm_campaign=activity_mailer%2Faction_taken&utm_medium=email&utm_source=causes#

12:58

Nov 27, 2015

 Sadhavi Khosla ✔
@sadhavi

 Follow

Parrikar was right when he said that @aamir_khan was taught a lesson as I had recvd this Whatsapp from BJP SM head.

8:12 PM - 31 Jul 2016 · Gurgaon, India, India

↩ ⇄ 259 ♥ 106

The Snapdeal petition following Aamir Khan's comments

71

possibly follow them. The one on Aamir became public because Manohar Parrikar confirmed it by calling it "our" smart team's but it had started with Shah Rukh and it continues to this day with Aamir's *Dangal* [to be released in December 2016], being trolled.'

Khosla's own tweet following Parrikar's statements:

I am a believer and my Hinduism has no room for such hate. If they go on like this they will destroy Hinduism. Even after winning they are only focused on polarizing and hate. I can't understand why we need to keep demonising Muslims and photoshop incendiary pictures. I have a young son. I don't want him to grow up in an India which is a mirror of Pakistan. I have dreams for him and I really want him to be a good person and not be infected with the virus of bigotry. My son is an American citizen. For the first time ever I am so scared at how we are turning on each other that I may move to the USA.

She decided she had to exit. Her husband had always kept aloof from politics but was hugely relieved by her decision. Khosla finally left the BJP social media cell at the end of 2015. She makes a face and says, 'You know I had so much vile hate in my phone from the BJP social media forwards that I felt cleansed after deleting them.'

Some of Khosla's WhatsApp messages

Here are a few WhatsApp messages that Khosla received from the social media cell. There were three kinds of messages – from her two contact points; from groups affiliated with the social media cell, such as the Hindu Defence League (HDL), which is followed by PM Modi on Twitter; and from Arvind Gupta directly.

Arvind Gupta directing the social media cell to tweet using #SansadChalneDo [let Parliament work] and (below) circulating a picture for use in anti-Gandhi propaganda

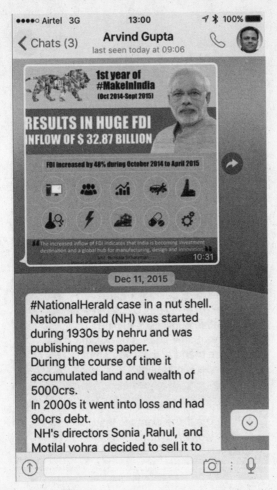

Arvind Gupta's WhatsApp messages about a Make in India campaign and on the National Herald *case in which the Gandhis are implicated*

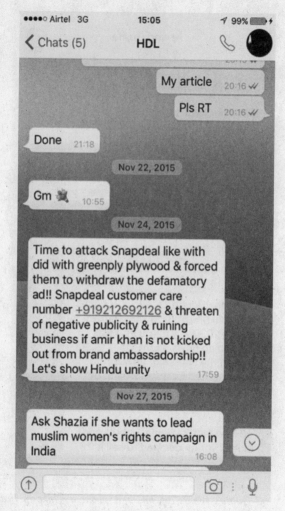

Attack on Snapdeal to drop Aamir as a brand ambassador – an instruction from the Hindu Defence League

More anti-Aamir material from HDL

3

I Am a Troll

Khosla was a passionate volunteer who was working for the party without pay. But the central BJP IT cell at Ashoka Road is also made up of what feels like a regular office-going crowd of 'techies', mostly young men from small engineering colleges who work through the regular 9-to-5 hours. Ankit Lal makes a critical distinction between AAP's and the BJP's social media workers. He claims that the AAP team is voluntary and works day and night. The BJP social media team on the other hand are normal working professionals. They fall silent after 9 p.m., after which social media is pretty much AAP territory. Khosla's account draws a clear picture of how they work. But who are they and what are they like?

I met over thirty young men and women who worked in the BJP social media cell and they spoke to me on condition of anonymity. They were initially introduced to me by BJP party members and seemed to be primarily men (and a few women) with solid Hindutva leanings. They fell in the age group of early twenties to late thirties. They seem to comprise the voter base that Modi once called the 'neo-middle class', born after the opening up of the Indian economy, who are above the poverty line but not yet middle class.

Author Chetan Bhagat fleshed out a troll in his column on 11 July 2015 in the *Times of India* where he described the Modi bhakts as 'exclusively male', with 'weak communication skills, especially in English', leading to an 'inferiority complex'. He also said they are 'generally not good at talking to women', they do desire women but can't get them and are therefore 'sexually frustrated'. Despite being overwhelmingly pro-Hindu they have an overriding sense of shame about being Hindu and speaking Hindi.

I felt that Bhagat's identity kit actually matched the BJP social media trolls I met. The one thing he did not mention was their near visceral hatred for Muslims.

They were all alarmingly tech savvy but had

poor to negligible English-speaking skills and appeared extremely frustrated that they were unable to communicate their views about Muslims and their plans to destroy the country.

You could also typecast their appearance. In standard issue Allen Solly trousers with the mandatory Indian male potbelly and checked shirt toting a black plastic laptop bag, he's the guy you would never look at again.

Troll 1

Troll 1 is in his late twenties. He orders coffee and is nervous and ill at ease. When I ask him to tell me about himself, he visibly relaxes and stops fidgeting with the sachets of sugar on the table. He tells me with huge pride that he's a Thakur from Pratapgarh in Uttar Pradesh. He had been the topper in his school and had sat for the engineering Joint Entrance Exam. Then his face darkens. 'I got 90 rank but these chamars [derogatory description of Dalits who work with leather] with 60 rank made it. I did not. Is this fair, madam? Everything for these people and the bloody Muslims.'

He's genuinely upset, reflective of the stagnant

state of the economy and the lack of job opportunities in Uttar Pradesh. He is heavily invested in Modi's vision of providing employment for India's burgeoning youth bulge; nearly 50 per cent of the population is below the age of twenty-five and more than 65 per cent below thirty-five.

I venture to point out that Muslims do not get reservations. He brushes it aside, saying 'that's because they don't study, too busy producing children'. When asked how he got involved with the BJP, he says, 'My family has always supported BJP. I was forced to go to Manav Rachna University which was very expensive but the only place which was offering me computer engineering. I got involved in student politics, campaigned for Modi ji. Madam, please realize he's the only leader who can change India, change the social order that has kept us down for years. All you people in the media don't know our history, our real sanskar. You only want to support Muslims.'

Every troll I met was clear about two things: Muslims are very violent and they are violent because they are non-vegetarian. If you try to dissuade them with data which establishes that

Muslims come off as the worst sufferers in communal riots, they don't want to listen.

Troll 1 keeps shaking his head, not making eye contact, not listening clearly. My arguments do not convince him. Then he looks up and says, 'You people don't want to actually help Muslims but just use anything to attack Modi ji.' This is a paradox I encountered continually through the investigations for this book. Modi is seen by his bhakt as both an avenger who will persecute those who have committed historical wrongs against them and simultaneously a man persecuted and victimized by the 'sickular' establishment.

Troll 1 then gets down to brass tacks. He says that they decide what should trend on social media with special hashtags being created each morning. Journalists, especially the high-profile ones who are deemed 'anti-Modi' or 'sickular presstitutes' representing 'paid media', are singled out for special attention of the abusive kind.

Troll 1 fidgets a bit, glugs his drink with a noisy gurgle and says, '*Ab aap se mil liya hoon toh kam gaali doonga.* I have watched you on TV, you not so bias [sic] [I will abuse you less now that I have met you. I have watched you on TV. You are not so biased].' Finally, as if offering a great concession, he mutters, 'I will only call you presstitute. Not prostitute or randi.'

I am very curious about why the attacks on women, particularly female journalists, are either rape threats, descriptions of exotic kinds of sexual acts they have performed, actual tweets of pubic hair with lurid descriptions of sex with the woman or how she needs to get a clean-up. The accounts which tweet the pubic hair pictures, if reported, are swiftly suspended by Twitter.

The troll squirms. Clearly it's easier to dish out abuse while being a keyboard warrior than to actually be questioned by a woman you've trolled. 'See, it's the easiest way because ordinary people don't know that it's an organized attack and it shocks people. Normally journalists block us immediately when we use sexual stuff. That's also a scoring point. We have a clear strike when you run away. I don't make rape threats and all; it's not right, but you people in the media are doing a lot of stuff. Affairs and free sex.

'*Aap ke media mein to sab log Pakistan se paisa lete hain. Uss Barkha Dutt koh dekhiye ISI agent hai. Uss ke toh Musalman miyan hain* [You people in the media take money from Pakistan. That Barkha Dutt is an ISI agent, she has a Pakistani husband],' he says.

Dutt is not married to a Pakistani and is a respected journalist. When asked how he knows these 'facts', Troll 1 smiles. Proud that he has scored, he says, 'All members of the social media cell are given a list of facts to attack you people with. We have screenshots of your controversial tweets which we use to attack you. Journalists who are corrupt, like Sagarika Ghose, who is a secret Christian, and her corrupt AAP-tard husband Rajdeep Sardesai, have made crores during the UPA acting as Radia dalals.' This is a reference to Nira Radia, the corporate lobbyist who was implicated in the UPA's 2G scandal.

His eyes gleam as he imparts a juicy morsel. 'I don't know how much their bungalow is worth but I always say 150 crores.' He adds, '*Par zyada phekna nahi chahiye* then people don't take so serious [You should not tell too many fibs or people won't take you seriously].'

He is much more circumspect on the subject of money. Was this trolling, which must be taking up a large part of his day, fungible? Did he get paid by the BJP? After ordering yet another frothy confection, he says, '*Arrey, kya Swati ji, hum log asli bhakt hai, ideology kei liye kartey hain* [we are true bhakts, and do the work for our ideology].'

But how does he manage to make a living? He looks around, lowers his voice and says, 'See, I am committed; *main karta hoon*. But others I have heard are looking for payments per tweet and even forming companies to get digital and social media campaigns of ministries.'

Troll 2

The most bigoted troll I meet is an obese young man who looks at least ten years older than he is. He is clearly uncomfortable talking to a woman and has only agreed to meet me after much persuasion from a former RSS worker. We meet near the RSS headquarters in Jhandewalan in Delhi and he immediately starts ranting about love jihad. When I argue back, saying the term has been cooked up to heat communal feeling, he looks at me as if I have lost my mind.

Without even pausing to get a second wind he asks if I've studied at a convent school. I try to say yes but only till primary school when he interrupts me to say, 'See, I could make out those nuns had brainwashed you. People like you have no idea of the reality of India. You don't know these Muslims and nuns just want to rule us again. Well, at least the nuns are not doing love jihad. Muslim men only want to corrupt Hindu women and have mixed breed children with them.'

He then goes off on a tangent. 'These Muslims are oversexed and their own women don't satisfy them so they go after ours. It's all the beef they eat.' Oversexed Muslims eating beef and going after poor, defenceless Hindu women. Feeling slightly sick after listening to his rant, I want to conclude the interview but he isn't having any of that. I get the feeling he has not had an audience in a long time.

He proceeds to list out several cases of love jihad he has been privy to. Sensing my lack of interest, he becomes aggressive and says, 'People like you are not really Indian so you don't care how much we suffer. You people are all funded by the West so you have to do their propaganda. You know we got real independence only when Modi ji became PM. Before that it was a fake independence. We had no respect in the world. Every country, including China, laughed at us. Now they all respect *virat* Bharat.'

As we part, he surreptitiously tries to take a picture of me. When I ask why, he says, 'Oh, because I have watched you on TV and my friends won't believe that I met you.' So I offer to pose for a selfie. After the picture is taken, he offers to send me some books which would correct my 'wrong perceptions'. Not keen to share my address, I try to wriggle out of this but he's strangely insistent, saying, 'I will come and give you the books.'

Troll 3

One of the most interesting trolls I meet is a young man from Bihar who had been a Janata Dal United (JDU) worker with Nitish Kumar when the BJP and the JDU were allies in the state government.

After Kumar quit the alliance on the issue of Mr Modi being the PM candidate, Troll 3 felt betrayed. He was aware of a shakha in his neighbourhood in Patna and started visiting it. There he was given a history lesson and a tiny amount of money to set up a small kiosk selling biscuits, gutka and water.

He tells me that after the alliance broke up, a small team would come from Delhi for two days every month to train the entire shakha on how to use social media. In Uttar Pradesh and Bihar, people who study in Hindi-medium schools use Rapidex English Speaking Course lessons, a primer to learn conversational English. This training was, he claims, virtually the 'Rapidex English course in social media'.

From never touching a computer – '*Mujhe darr lagta tha kahin kharab na kar doon* [I was scared I might damage it]' – to being taught the basics of the keyboard by first using the shakha's dilapidated old typewriter and overcoming the disadvantage of having been schooled in Bihar's education system where copying is the norm, Troll 3 has come a long way.

'First they used to try and teach the entire shakha but lots of older people did not want to learn so they selected a core group and basically even re-taught us ABCD.' Blushing a bright fire-engine red, he says, 'They even taught us the Hindi lipi. As you know, in Bihar we talk a lot of politics but basics weak hota hai [They even re-taught us the basic Hindi script. As you know in Bihar we talk a lot of politics but our basics of learning are weak].

'Madam, using a computer is so easy and gives me so much power. All the lies that are told in the name of education in India I can expose. When lies are tweeted by the *vamphanti* [leftists] in Nitish's support, I can stop them by attacking the liars. *Har issue pe hamara line hota hai* [We have a line on every issue] and I manage my booth, go to the shakha and help my party. The way I am going, I hope to get an MLA ticket in the next five years. I would have got nothing if I had stayed with Nitish. He would only promote Lalu's parivar. Modi ji has given all of us in the Sangh hope.'

For Troll 3, working for the BJP in this capacity in Bihar, where young people had few economic opportunities, was a way to get ahead. He could have gone either way ideologically but, simply put, this ideology provided opportunity.

When asked if he actually believes the stuff he tweets to his nearly 15,000 followers, he looks sheepish and says, 'What I did not learn in school I learned in the shakha. *Aur belief kya hota hai? Har umar pe badalta hai* [What is belief? It changes with every age]. When I had no money I hated shopkeepers because I could afford nothing. Now with my booth I want protection for what I earn.' He said, '*Hum Bihari hamesha politics mein interest rakhtey hai lekin ab Modi ji ko defend karna mushkil ho gaya hai. Bahut boltey hai, lekin on-ground kuch nahi hai* [We Biharis are always interested in politics but it's become tough to defend Modi ji. He speaks a lot but nothing is happening on the ground].'

He has insisted on meeting me at a tiny eatery in Delhi's North Campus, where he stays with his relatives while visiting from Patna. Pointing to the stinking garbage lying around in piles, with dirty cows poking desultorily through it and flies buzzing around, he finally smiles a real smile which reaches his eyes and says, '*Madam, yeh asliat hai; kitna Singapore bataogey?* [This is the reality. How will you claim it is Singapore?].

'*Umeed bahut hai lekin hoh nahi paa raha is liye aaj kal main bhi gaali kam deta hoon. Kya faayda?* [There is a lot of hope but it does not seem to be happening. So now I also abuse less. What is the point?].'

4

Some Other Trends

The accounts of these social media cell workers provide a vivid picture of how the NDOC works on a day-to-day basis and shed light on some of their high-profile social media campaigns. In this chapter we look at some other worrying trends in online behaviour.

Thailand connection

Ankit Lal, the AAP social media chief, has replicated the BJP's social media cell, and he tracks the ruling party's social media as part of his work. He shared with me an investigation (see Appendix B) he did using analytics tools, which was also reviewed and confirmed by Siddharth Bhaskar, an independent UK-based technical expert who runs his own consulting firm. Bhaskar is an information technology engineer with an MBA from a leading European business school. He has worked in India, the US and Europe with top consulting and IT firms including Hughes, Accenture and PwC. In his most recent roles he has helped senior management at FTSE 100 firms as well as UK public sector enterprises. He is currently running his own consulting firm that uses technology to help clients make better business decisions.

Lal's study shows that Twitter handles in Thailand regularly tweeted with BJP-created Modi hashtags. The Thailand hashtags have even been used by Mr Modi, Manohar Parrikar, Smriti Irani and Rajnath Singh.

Lal says there are two possible explanations for this. The BJP social media control centres could have started using virtual private networks (VPNs) to hide their location and identity. A VPN is a private network which extends across a public network or the Internet. It enables users to send and receive data while pretending they are directly connected to a particular network or geography. Simply put, VPNs can hide the actual location of a user. For example, they can be used by someone based in Delhi to pretend that their computer is in London so they can access content that is only available to UK-based users. Hiding behind a VPN wall, fake handles are created to trend politically motivated hashtags. This may explain the use of identical content by multiple handles.

The other possible explanation is that the BJP has hired a marketing agency in Thailand to do their online work. This includes using fake handles and abusing leaders of other parties, such as Arvind Kejriwal, with hashtags like #UdtaKejriwalfundsUdtaPunjab. The details of the heat maps identified by Lal are available in Appendix B. When Modi was in Mexico, Suphan Buri, a small town in central Thailand located 101 kilometres north of Bangkok, was in fourth spot among places tweeting about the visit. Lal rather cheekily calls it 'Modi ji's Thailand connection'.

Companies as targets

E-commerce giant Myntra has also been attacked online. It all started when Gita S. Kapoor, a member of BJP's Women's Wing of Andheri, West Mumbai – 'passionate about women empowerment' according to her Twitter bio – tweeted an image that showed Lord Krishna ordering a sari from Myntra while Dushasana disrobes Draupadi in the background.

The Myntra advertisement which attracted a swarm of Twitter trolls

Kapoor, who has a huge number of followers, tweeted an open threat on 25 August 2016 to Myntra

Gita S. Kapoor @GitaSKapoor
.*@myntra* kindly explain or go the amazon/snapdeal way.

The image had been made nearly six months earlier by Scroll Droll, a social media publication famous for interesting graphic cards. For this project, they had imagined mythological characters using modern facilities. So Krishna uses the Myntra app to get an extra-long sari. Shiva waits for a cab and uses the Uber app. Lord Ganesha uses Zomato to order food while sage Narada uses the travel portal Yatra.

A hashtag began trending asking for a boycott of Myntra's products. Myntra, terrified by what had transpired with Snapdeal after Aamir Khan's comments, tried explaining that the graphic was made by a third party without their consent or knowledge but the trolls turned a deaf ear. Scroll Droll also tweeted, 'This poster was created by us in Feb. We removed it immediately as we never intended to hurt sentiments.'

Myntra ✓
@myntra

⚙   **Follow**

We did not create this artwork nor do we endorse this.

> **ScrollDroll** @ScrollDroll
> We take up the responsibility of this artwork. Myntra is nowhere associated with it directly or indirectly. (2/2) twitter.com/GitaSKapoor/st...

Myntra's response and Scroll Droll's clarification

Online trolls relied on their strategy of targeting Myntra as they had done with Snapdeal by giving the app a low rating. @ProudlySayGujju tweeted on August 26:

> Downloaded Myntra app and gave 1star and asked "Unconditional apologies" and deleted app. Downgrade Myntra. Show our Power..#BoycottMyntra

> **Abs Indian** @ROFL_India
> Hey @*myntra* plz make fun of other religions similarly.. They wud make u pee in ur pants..so will we. *#BoycottMyntra*

This was then tweeted on promoted hashtag #BoycottMyntra and the identical text was used in hundreds of tweets that followed.

> *#BoycottMyntra* this is the price you have to pay if you keep on mocking Hinduism just on the name of Democracy!!

'Forty-rupee tweets'

Agencies are now also being paid to tweet and trend hashtags that attack anti-BJP parties. I managed to get one such memo from an agency which is being paid to tweet against Arvind Kejriwal at the rate of forty rupees for seven tweets – although who is making the payment remains unclear.

The document is reproduced below.

From: Pari C <twcampaigns@gmail.com>

Date: Thu, Sep 8, 2016 at 11:20 AM

Subject: #KejriKeHeere Activity

To:

Hello Friends,

You are shortlisted for today's activity going live at   11:30 AM sharp... (8th of Sept)

Brief:

This is to protest against corrupt ministers of AAP Party

Please follow the time slot (Strictly follow the timing - Not all the tweets in one go)

11:30 AM   to   11:45 AM   -   5 tweets

12:00 PM   to   12:30 PM   -   2 tweet

Hashtag   -   #KejriKeHeere (in every tweet)

Objective   -   Trending..

Payment   -   40 Rs.

Total tweets -   7

Sample tweets. You can copy paste but modify a little :)

AAP has become the country's top most party having majority of criminal leaders. #KejriKeHeere

Two MLAs facing serious charges, including those of molestation, cheating and forgery arrested #KejriKeHeere

Women's security is a primary thing to implement, but i guess AK is least bothered. #KejriKeHeere

AAP is full of people ready to take advantage of your sentiments and suffering. #KejriKeHeere

What are #KejriKeHeere doing?

Will #KejriKeHeere run the government like this?

#KejriKeHeere is a big question!

I am hearing of #KejriKeHeere all around. What is the truth?

#KejriKeHeere is all over media. What is the truth?

We need at least people who respect women! #KejriKeHeere don't and it is sad!

#KejriKeHeere and their stories are all around. What is really happening?

Where are the real #KejriKeHeere

Why was SomnathBharti allowed to target African women late at night that too without any lady police? #KejriKeHeere @htTweets

Kejriwal says No corruption in delhi as he and his minister sips chai and eat samosas worth 1 crore #KejriKeHeere

AAP wants to spoil the atmosphere of Punjab. #KejriKeHeere

Arvind Kejriwal is the only minister in the country who can have his cake and eat it too! #KejriKeHeere

Arrest of Naresh Yadav shows that AAP

is working on directions of anti-national forces #KejriKeHeere @thetribunechd

Kejriwal promised to end corruption but not from his party. #KejriKeHeere @ArvindKejriwal @AamAadmiParty @ndtv

Where is the dignity and honesty of the Kejriwal govt that we the public of Delhi voted for? Shame #KejriKeHeere @ArvindKejriwal

Fake degree, molester, wife beater, sex scandal, rapist etc in @AamAadmiParty #KejriKeHeere

Why you are adding corrupt leaders to @AamAadmiParty @ArvindKejriwal @JagbaniOnline #KejriKeHeere

RT and Favorite will not be considered and Tweets After 12:30 PM will not be counted

Payment will be cleared in 30 Days from today!

Thanks.

Regards,

Pari C (@D_KohlEyedChic)

TWCampaigns.com is a domain registered in Hyderabad but there is no website. Pari C

(@D_KohlEyedChic) describes herself as a digital influencer and blogger. She blogs and tweets about various brands. AAP countered the anti-Kejriwal tweets by trending a hashtag #bhaktssellforRs40.

BJP social media workers in the government?

There are indications that some of the BJP social media cell members might be working within the Government of India or trying to gain contracts.

Minister for Women and Child Development Maneka Gandhi was approached by a group of people referred to by the BJP as being active on social media and followed by the PM – i.e., members of the BJP's social media cell. They asked Gandhi to give them the contract to run her ministry's newly minted social media account.

The minister said that the normal tendering process would be followed. Following the transparent bidding process, the lowest bidder, PR professional Dilip Cherian's company Perfect Relations, was awarded the contract. A huge outcry ensued on social media. Hashtags were created and dark conspiracy theories bandied about. Gandhi was forced to cancel the contract.

I asked Cherian about it. He was circumspect and said, 'We believe in providing best value at the best price when it comes to winning large contracts, both public and private. We follow the same principle for even smaller contracts and our effort is always to be L1. We win some, we lose some.'

Despite the contract with Cherian's company being cancelled, an anon Twitter account, Vande Matram, who tweets at @UnsubtleDesi and is followed by Modi, tweeted on 26 August 2016:

> Dynasty hack from your party who hired Cherian @BJP.India thnks [sic] journos on Twitter for whatsapp wishes. R u stupid not to see why she's pulling?

Another aide who came into the public spotlight earlier this year was Shilpi Tewari, who worked with HRD minister Smriti Irani. Irani had asked that Tewari be hired as a 'consultant' by her ministry in the position of social media expert even though she lacked the necessary qualifications. Forensic reports commissioned by the Delhi government alleged that Tewari was behind the doctoring of videos that sent student leader Kanhaiya Kumar to Tihar Jail for nearly a month. Tewari certainly circulated the 'morphed' Kanhaiya video on Twitter and later suspended the account from where she had shared it. She was back after a hiatus, denying all allegations. She currently describes herself as an 'ex-BJP volunteer'.

Careless talk

Some of the government's official social media communication has in the past year been troubling, mirroring the strategies of the BJP's social media cell – photoshopping images, making false claims and tweeting hate messages.

The culture ministry, led by billionaire Dr Mahesh Sharma, recently photoshopped an Indian flag on a Pakistani jet in an Independence Day video.

The culture ministry's verified Twitter handle released the video on 12 August 2016. Titled '70 years of Independence', it showed two JF-17

Thunder planes flying with what looked like a badly photoshopped Indian flag on them.

The irony is that the Pakistan air force's JF-17 Thunder, also known as the Chinese air force's FC-1 Xiaolong (Fierce Dragon), is a multi-role combat aircraft developed jointly by the Pakistan Aeronautical Complex and the Chengdu Aircraft Corporation of China. The culture ministry's video was meant to 'promote an online system for construction applications' made to the Indian National Monuments Authority. The safeguarding of monuments is part of the mandate of the ministry and the online system is meant to enhance this.

Even China's official news agency, Xinhua, took a swipe at India from its verified Twitter handle, posting both pictures and tweeting: 'In goof-up, India uses Pakistani fighter jets in video marking 70th Independence Day.' After the customary outcry on Twitter, the ministry simply pulled down the video without any explanation.

The Press Information Bureau (PIB), the nodal communication wing of the Government of India, is another body that has photoshopped PM Modi's pictures. All images issued by the

PIB are regarded as official images of the PM. An unforgettable image showed PM Modi surveying flood-ravaged Chennai from a helicopter. Well and good, except for the tiny fact that the PIB had photoshopped the view from the helicopter's window. A huge outcry followed and the PIB came up with the convoluted explanation that it had 'not photoshopped the pictures but only merged them'.

The prime minister's speech on Independence Day 2016 from the ramparts of the Red Fort contained a lie about the electrification of a village in Uttar Pradesh. PM Modi claimed that the village, Nagla Fatela, finally had electricity after seventy years, saying, 'Nagla Fatela is just three hours from Delhi but Delhi took seventy years to send electricity to it.'

Power Minister Piyush Goyal tweeted pictures of Nagla Fatela villagers watching the PM's address. The gram panchayat immediately denied the claim, saying the pictures were not of their village and they did not have any electricity. The PMO's official handle had also tweeted the speech. The government deleted the photographs and the tweets after the scandal.

Response to PM Modi's remarks on Nagla Fatela village

These may not be deliberate, carefully told lies; indeed there's a larger possibility that they are a result of careless errors. The problem of course is that the government's carelessness has enormous implications. What does it mean for the Government of India to be spreading false images of its work? Inappropriate language also shows up on verified, official Twitter handles of the government and its allied bodies.

@startupIndia is a verified blue-ticked official handle of the Ministry of Commerce and Industry. Recently, it retweeted an anonymous troll 'who wanted the Army to kill all presstitutes'. When this was first pointed out to Arvind Gupta, he claimed that the 'tweets were photoshopped'. However, after widespread outrage, the tweets were deleted and an apology offered from the handle. Union Minister of State for Commerce and Industry Nirmala Sitharaman also said that the 'employee had been sacked'.

A verified handle of the high-profile Digital India project of the GOI tweeted a poem on 8 September 2016 which said that the mass murder of Kashmiris was the 'height of patriotism'. This is a tax-funded GOI handle. The poem also said,

A verified handle of the Government of India retweets an anonymous troll making threats to journalists

'Thrash them all you want, Army, break their bones: If Mehbooba calls the police: Modi will handle it.' In what has fast become the norm, the tweet was deleted following the customary outrage. The telecom ministry simply said it had outsourced the management of the official Twitter account to digital marketing company Trivone.

In the first week of September 2016, All India Radio's official handle tweeted about Rahul Gandhi, asking

> Why he got scared earlier? How he became daring again to defame #RSS.. He should stick to comments #RahulRattlesRSS

Gandhi had claimed that the RSS had killed Mahatma Gandhi for which the RSS had filed a defamation case against him.

On 9 September the verified handle of the Ministry of Railways retweeted a tweet calling Delhi Chief Minister Arvind Kejriwal a liar.

Sometimes this has a funny side. Irani, as textile minister, started an #Iwearhandlooms hashtag to promote handlooms, setting the campaign off with a picture of herself wearing a handloom sari. Unfortunately the verified official handle seemed to be managed by a bot which started mindless bot praise of anyone putting up a picture claiming to be wearing handlooms. Twitter had a laugh with pictures of Baba Ramdev and even PM Modi wearing a sari getting automated bot praise which read 'Your #Iwearhandlooms look will go a long way in supporting the weaver community in India'.

The bigger picture

As I have continually argued, the real danger occurs when the online hate generated by trolls results in offline violence. Take once again the case of student leader Kanhaiya Kumar. Kumar was first put in custody for a doctored video in early 2016. Then he and the journalists covering his bail proceedings were brutally beaten up at Patiala House by lawyers who claimed allegiance to the BJP. Fighting also broke out outside Patiala House.

The video, as mentioned earlier, was allegedly doctored by Shilpi Tewari, close aide of then-HRD minister Smriti Irani. Tewari had even assisted Irani during the Amethi campaign. One of the assaulters that day was BJP's Delhi MLA O.P. Sharma, a close associate of Finance Minister Arun Jaitley. Sharma claimed that he had assaulted a man outside Patiala House because he was shouting anti-India slogans. Reporters present at the court say the man was shouting anti-Arun Jaitley slogans.

Sharma and the band of law-breaking lawyers were feted like heroes and they gave a series of interviews before Sharma made a cursory visit to a police station where he was offered tea and biscuits and told that he was free to go. The Hindu Legal Cell tweeted from its handle:

> we support and congratulate the Nationalists Advocates who have beaten up Azfal supporter JNU students outside Patiala House Court.

The perfect merger of online hate and offline violence. Worse, while Kumar was arrested on the basis of doctored videos, the Delhi Police took no action against the masked men who actually shouted the anti-India slogans in JNU. Kumar was not one of them. Sources say that the Delhi Police has identified the group but not arrested anyone.

During the events, #shutdownJNU was trending on Twitter. In a farcical aside Gyandev Ahuja, a BJP MLA from Ramgarh, Rajasthan, said he had counted the number of used condoms and liquor bottles in JNU's garbage and that this established the university as a 'den of debauchery and free love'.

Upping the ante, Union Home Minister Rajnath Singh mistakenly cited a parody handle of Pakistani militant leader Hafiz Saeed and used it to accuse him of supporting Kumar.

Speaking to reporters, Rajnath Singh said, 'Unfortunate that the JNU incident has been supported by LeT chief Hafiz Saeed. The nation must also accept the reality that the incident that took place in JNU has been supported by LeT chief Hafiz Saeed. Nobody should try to achieve political benefits from such incidents. I have given clear instruction that strict action must be taken against anyone who's found guilty but innocent people must not be harassed.'

The real Saeed immediately responded: 'Alleging me for #JNU protest based on a Fake account in my name is a prime example of how Indian government fools its own people.' This was tweeted from the handle @HafizSaeedLive on 14 February 2016.

Singh does not carry a cellphone and his Twitter account is handled by the Ministry of Home Affairs. Not content with this embarrassment,

Some Other Trends

Tweets   Media   Likes

Hafeez Muhamad Saeed @Ha... 20h
We proudly invite all JNU
Students to Pakistan & request
them to continue their Pro-
Kashmiri, Anti-Indian Propaganda
in our Universities.

↩   ⟲ 4   ♥ 2

Hafeez Muhamad Saeed @Ha... 20h
Those JNU students of Delhi who
are facing problem in India should
come to Pakistan & continue your
study here in Punjab Uni with
Dignity.

↩   ⟲ 8   ♥ 4

Hafeez Muhamad Saeed @Haf... 1d
We request our Pakistani Brothers
to trend #SupportJNU for our
pro-Pakistani JNUites brothers.
#PakStandWithJNU

Tweets from the fake handle of Hafiz Saeed

the ministry then responded with the following statement on Twitter, which was picked on by the rabid right wing as a signal to target JNU: 'Anyone who raises anti-India slogans will not be spared.'

Tweet from the Twitter handle of Delhi Police

Some Other Trends

LAHORE: Hafiz Saeed, the mastermind of the 26/11 Mumbai terror attack, has rejected claims by Home Minister Rajnath Singh that he had supported the controversial event at Delhi's Jawaharlal Nehru University in memory of Parliament attack convict Afzal Guru.

"The India home minister has alleged that I am behind the protest of Kashmiri students in Jawaharlal Nehru University where they chanted slogans in favour of Pakistan. He also talked my tweet in this regard. I felt strange after learning the Indian home minister had given a reference of a tweet with my name," Hafiz Saeed said in a video message posted on YouTube on Monday.

"Neither I am behind the students protest nor I did any tweet to incite them (students). It is a fake tweet. India has made an issue out of this as if I am behind this protest campaign," said Hafiz Saeed, who tops the list of India's most-wanted terrorists.

"The Indian minister is misleading his own people and the world by levelling allegation on me that I am behind this protest campaign," he added.

On Sunday, the Home Minister linked the founder of terror group Lashkar-e-Taiba to the student demonstrations that saw anti-India slogans being shouted at an on-campus event that went ahead despite JNU denying it permission. "The incident at JNU has received support from Hafiz Saeed. This is a truth that the nation needs to understand," Mr Singh had said.

Mr Singh's remarks generated a fierce backlash. Hours later, the Home Ministry issued a clarification that the remarks were based on "inputs from different agencies".

The ministry clarification also followed reports that Mr Singh and the police were misled by a tweet purportedly from a Twitter handle in the name of Hafiz Saeed. On Sunday, Pakistani newspaper The Dawn reported the Hafiz Saeed handle was fake. Hafiz Saeed's Twitter handle was blocked a long time ago.

Hafiz Saeed's clarification regarding the events at JNU

5

Returning to the Roots:
The RSS Link

A larger question can be asked as we near the end of our investigation. Is there something particular about the BJP DNA that makes it more receptive to the darker side of the social media world? I would argue yes, and give two possible reasons.

Firstly, the roots of the current BJP social media cell lie in the election campaign of 2014 and the preparation that began for it many years earlier. As Sadhavi Khosla says, the social media cell seems to be on a permanent war footing, not wholly accepting that the election campaign is over. BJP minister Nitin Gadkari made a similar comment when talking about the party as a whole. Being in this constant campaign mode might explain some of the ugliness generated by the social media cell.

The other factor is possibly the RSS being the original trainer of the BJP in the use of social media. This originated from a group of swayamsevaks from Tamil Nadu, who were all techies in the early days of social media in the new millennium and who started using it as a means to communicate with each other. They were led by Ram Madhav, fulltime RSS pracharak and an electrical engineer from Andhra University, now on secondment to the BJP as one of its most powerful general secretaries.

Madhav went from shakha to shakha training them after convincing a reluctant RSS that it was a powerful communication tool and not mere 'fashion'. The core group of techies was based in Pune and most of them remain there. But the main operations spread to Bangalore, India's IT capital, where all the RSS's IT needs are still serviced. I spoke to Madhav (interview reproduced below) and an original techie from the group.

The RSS has been banned four times in its history (in 1947 in the Punjab province of British India; after Mahatma Gandhi's assassination in 1948; during the Emergency between 1975 and 1977; and after the demolition of Babri Masjid in 1992). A sense of persecution and insecurity thus runs in the organization's make-up; its structure is geared towards secrecy and is cell-based. It was natural then that a well-developed and efficient way of working with social media would emerge from it. And one can also argue that this sense of persecution and insecurity can be seen in the BJP's current social media strategy.

Veteran editor and former MP H.K. Dua has covered the Sangh for nearly forty years as a reporter and editor of the *Times of India*, *Indian Express* and *Hindustan Times*. He told me, 'One thing about the Sangh is that they are remarkably adaptable. And rumour campaigns are their forte; they excel in them. Always have. The medium may have changed but I doubt the message has.'

Ankit Lal told me that it was this group of techies from the RSS who laid out the blueprint for the BJP's infamous social media cell. The training continues even now and Madhav continues to address IT shakhas. With the technology advantage added to the RSS's already formidable ground presence, BJP got the edge in the propaganda war against an already faltering UPA.

I spoke to one of the original RSS techies from Madurai, Chennai. He was in his late fifties, had studied chemical engineering from IIT Kanpur and spoke fluent Hindi. He was very soft-spoken and his large eyes lit up with mirth as he talked with me. 'Technology is ideology neutral,' he told me. 'I believe in the Sangh's values so I volunteered the time and trained them. What they do with the training I may not necessarily approve of. But this was our way of countering leftist propaganda, which is equally bad.'

Like Arvind Gupta, the Chennai swayamsevak felt very strongly that mainstream media and the key institutions in the country were dominated by the left and its ideas. It was only through social media that the RSS could find a way to reach people.

Interview with Ram Madhav

Ram Madhav is one of the most powerful general secretaries of the BJP. Wearing an Apple watch on his wrist and sitting in front of a wafer-thin Apple computer on his desk, he meets me in his smart office in New Delhi. He is the mastermind of the original Chennai project and smilingly admits to me that it was his idea to build the secret IT shakhas. Madhav convinced the Sangh that using social media would give them an edge in refining communications and targeting supporters. Initially he held workshops in shakhas to encourage the use of social media. He was also responsible for the Narendra Modi app and the use of WhatsApp to further refine communication. I reproduce here his interview.

As one of the original architects of the organized use of social media, tell me how it happened.
See, you remember the new media technology has helped organizations, parties and leaders to directly connect with the constituents. The people you want to connect with do not need any intermediary now. Technology has given you an opportunity to directly connect with them. We realized this power of the technology.

When did you realize this power?
Right from the time these things came in. I was one of the persons who used to argue in my organization that the RSS shouldn't look at this as something that was just fashionable. Things that are fashionable today will become part of

your daily routine tomorrow. There was a time when even refrigerators were a luxury. Today every house has them.

It's perceived that you use social media to bypass mainstream media.
Well, nobody should think we are trying to bypass mainstream media or that it is less important. Mainstream media has its own role and its own impact which no political party can afford to ignore. If we do it we must be living in [a] fool's paradise. But, having said it, this new alternative is providing us with an opportunity to connect with the masses directly.

Is there a feeling in the RSS and the BJP that mainstream media is hostile to them and to counter it you are using social media?
[Long pause] Biases exist. They reflect in society and mainstream media is a reflection of society. But, today I feel that by using social media I am reaching out to my target group. Many people don't even realize it but we are slowly integrating it with our election work. We have a hundred million

members in my party. We are now carrying out an exercise where we are mapping how many of these party members are Facebook users. Eighty million are FB users. I will use FB to directly connect with my karyakarta.

The perception of the RSS is that it's a traditional organization, very suspicious of and resistant to change. Did it take a lot of effort for you to convince them?

Initially there was a feeling that for organizations like the RSS, social media was not needed, but then some of us convinced the organization that we should use the technology. That it was a very big facilitator.

But say for example Dr Mohan Bhagwat, the RSS chief, does he understand social media? Is he on Twitter or FB? Does he look through timelines and all that?

He is a regular follower of media content through technology. I mean he uses his own iPad to look at things and all that. Probably he is not there on FB and Twitter, etc. but RSS is there.

When did Project Social Media take off for the RSS?

We have run programmes for karyakartas since the early 2000s. I remember running three-day workshops in Pune. In those days Pune was the technology hub. We ran programmes for managing websites. Websites were the big thing.

Now for the elephant in the room. The BJP has a huge social media cell. A lot of people – journalists and ordinary people – feel attacked by the trolls who owe allegiance to the cell and they feel that you, the BJP, are facilitating these attacks.

Look [for the first time very defensively during this interview], the BJP encouraging trolls is totally rubbish. We ourselves have been the victims of trolling. Look, this is a universal hazard for some very prominent people on social media, but to blame any one party or any one cell is not correct. I would only say everyone is a victim. I know sometimes women face huge problems of rape threats. I feel very bad seeing the kind of things that are written. I would disagree vociferously with others on social media but I draw the line at personal attacks. Sadly for you journalists, it's a professional hazard. My own feeling is that in a medium where abuse is so rampant that medium will die faster.

Are you seriously telling me there is no organized trolling by the BJP? Many journalists including me have been attacked by handles followed by the PM.

One thing we have to understand, that every hard criticism is not trolling. Somebody is attacking you in very strong words that does not mean he is a troll.

Come on, Ram, you have a minister calling journalists 'presstitutes'. As a journalist I am very offended and so are all journalists. Do you think a minister in the GOI and a senior party leader should be talking like this?

[*Fumbles*] There is no exact meaning of the word 'presstitute'. If it is offensive, let us all decide not to use it. I am not supporting that word. But these are some of the professional hazards you face.

It's a very loaded term – why use it?
All right, I don't use it.

But no other party – the Congress or AAP, who are also on social media – goes around calling well-known journalists 'presstitutes' so why does BJP? It's BJP specific. So what does the BJP say about it?
I don't want to say much about it. I have never used it and will never use it. As you rightly said it's a loaded word, better avoid it than try and explain why you used it.

The RSS has a lot of techies. Has that helped your enormous social media edge?
Absolutely nobody knows this but initially all our in-house technology needs were met by our shakha people from Bangalore. The first IT shakha was started in Bangalore, the IT capital of India.

When you say IT shakha, what do you mean?
IT shakha is where the IT professionals come together. The concept was developed in early 2001; it was a very progressive thing. It's not the normal shakha that you see in the parks, with people

exercising. The IT shakhas are not necessarily held in open grounds. Maybe if there is an IT company with ten to fifteen guys, sometimes girls, they will hold the shakha in the canteen, have a discussion about national issues. They are our people.

And I would go and have a chat with them. I used to go and get five or six of them together and hold discussions with them. The interesting part is that girls also participated. Now it is there in all the centres. In fact, Gurgaon has a lot of IT shakhas. This is the most interesting arm of the RSS, the IT arm.

Have you already moved on to WhatsApp, with the promise of an even more targeted audience, from the echo chamber of Twitter?

Yes, of course, and apps. Through my app I can reach out to eighty million people. Then it makes complete sense to me. Now in every party meeting we ensure that we open a stall and our people download the Modi app, so millions download it. So why should I have Twitter, I may as well have the Modi app. And we say, see the Modi app and then post on social media.

Are you fostering a cult of Modi?
No, no. We are fostering the cult of GOI work.
Modi happens to be the PM. Even RSS is
developing its app through which it will put its
lectures, etc., online.

Conclusion

The BJP has the country's most impressive social media cell compared to any other political party. They, along with the RSS, took advantage of new technologies earlier than anyone. Social media suited the needs, personality and history of these organizations, who felt they had always been excluded by mainstream media. This early attention to social media was one of the factors behind their extraordinary electoral victory of 2014. Today this cell is made up of a tight, efficient group of paid engineers, party workers and volunteers.

But these 'yodhas' wage a darker battle – against journalists who hold opposing views, minority communities like Muslims and Dalits, and opposition parties. This kind of fight is ugly, its weapons are vicious language, sex-filled imagery, outrageous lies and doctored photographs and videos.

What's especially troubling about India is that these voices and behaviours have entered the very heart of power. PM Modi follows a number of the chief offenders on Twitter, the BJP social media cell has waged battles against prominent actors for voicing concern against intolerance, student leaders from opposition parties have been thrown into jail because of doctored videos, verified accounts within the government have tweeted communal and hate speeches, and prominent ministers have begun to use some of this offensive language in public.

I am fearful too of the way social media amplifies caste and communal tensions, especially after the incident in Una, Gujarat, where seven young Dalit men were flogged for skinning a dead cow in a slow, orgiastic ritual of violence filmed and uploaded by the offenders on social media; the lynching of Mohammad Akhlaq in Dadri; the trending of a fake Hindu exodus from Kairana; and Modi bhakts sharing Pakistan videos on cow slaughter to incite riots. In the following years, the Modi–Shah duo have three important elections, including the mother of all battles in Uttar Pradesh, to win. Modi wants a second term as well. These aims will give the party more occasions and reasons to stir up tension. The social media skirmishes will play a crucial role in this regard.

What will the future hold? More bad news, I fear. The BJP's social media cell has the potential to morph into a bigger monster as it attacks citizens for not conforming to the party's world view on issues like diet, religion, Kashmir and tribal rights. It's time we opened our eyes to the dangers ahead.

Appendices

Appendix A

Trolls Followed by
PM Narendra Modi

	Name	Handle
1.	Rishi Bagree	@rishibagree
2.	Gita S. Kapoor	@GitaSKapoor
3.	Mahaveer	@MahaveerM_
4.	Gaurav Pradhan	@DrGPradhan
5.	Rahul Raj	@bhak_sala
6.	Mirror of India	@anilkapur_
7.	Amit Shah Army	@AmitShahArmy
8.	Who slapped whom	@bwoyblunder
9.	Ankit (in Hindi)	@indiantweeter
10.	Nikunj Sahu	@NikunjSahu

Name	Handle
11. Gitika [in Hindi]	@ggiittiikkaa
12. Tajinder Pal Singh Bagga	@TajinderBagga
13. Suresh Nakhua	@sureshnakhua
14. Hindu Defence League	@HDLindiaOrg
15. Hindu Defence League	@HDL_Global
16. Niraj #HDL	@Nir_27
17. harshkushwaha #HDL	@harshkushwaha10
18. MaHak #HDL	@mahakbhawani
19. Shilpi Tewari	@shilpitewari
20. Priti Gandhi	@MrsGandhi
21. Prashant	@VAJR
22. Anil Kohli	@anilkohli54
23. AshDebey_	@AshDubey_
24. Saint ChopdaSaab	@Chopdasaab
25. Bharat_Mata_ki_Jay	@Nations_Choice
26. Rahul Roushan	@Rahulroushan

Note: This list was accurate at the time of sending the book to press

Appendix B

I work for AAP: This is what tracking BJP on Twitter revealed to me

Ankit Lal's report (reproduced with thanks from DailyO)

ANKIT LAL
@ankitlal

As a member of the Aam Aadmi Party (AAP), and as someone who has led its social media team for three elections, I have had to monitor BJP's social media strategy closely.

In all, we have come twice on top of them. Once

during 2013 and then again in 2015, but in 2014 they squarely beat us.

In the past few months though, I have been more involved with working on some long-term projects for the party. I am also working on a book on Indian social media, besides running my consultancy business.

Yet, I find always time to be on Twitter. I think tweeting is my forte and I can't deny that I don't enjoy it.

More recently, I have noticed that the BJP has changed its social media strategy. Some of their old and committed supporters on Twitter also seem to have gone silent.

In fact, whenever they start tweeting against Aam Aadmi Party or Arvind Kejriwal, I find multiple users are mostly using the same content. Some news portals have also pointed this out.

A few evenings ago, my partner-in-crime, Charanjeet, and I were sitting and chatting after a long day at work. While Charan was playing with one of our data analytics tools, our respected Prime Minister Narendra Modi was visiting Qatar, and #ModiInQatar was the number one trend in India on Twitter.

Appendix B

rupinderjeet singh @happylakhewal · 6m
If Udta Punjab gives bad name to Punjab it is good that Censor board has asked to made the cuts. #UdtaKejriFundsUdtaPunjab

Ruchika Sharma @Ruchika861 · 10m
If Udta Punjab gives bad name to Punjab it is good that Censor board has asked to made the cuts. #UdtaKejriFundsUdtaPunjab

SukhMan Singh @SukhMan1122 · 28m
If Udta Punjab gives bad name to Punjab it is good that Censor board has asked to made the cuts. #UdtaKejriFundsUdtaPunjab

Bittu @BittuKhaira · 34m
If Udta Punjab gives bad name to Punjab it is good that Censor board has asked to made the cuts. #UdtaKejriFundsUdtaPunjab @DebashishHITs

Satnam singh @SatnamRai25 · 38m
If Udta Punjab gives bad name to Punjab it is good that Censor board has asked to made the cuts. #UdtaKejriFundsUdtaPunjab

Jasmail @Jasmail12 · 40m
If Udta Punjab gives bad name to Punjab it is good that Censor board has asked to made the cuts. #UdtaKejriFundsUdtaPunjab

Sukhmeet Kaur @Sukhmeet2424 · 42m
If Udta Punjab gives bad name to Punjab it is good that Censor board has asked to made the cuts. #UdtaKejriFundsUdtaPunjab

Sukh Deep Kaur @kaur_sukhi2 · 43m
If Udta Punjab gives bad name to Punjab it is good that Censor board has asked to made the cuts. #UdtaKejriFundsUdtaPunjab

When he keyed #ModiInQatar into our tool, he found something peculiar at play. It's a bit technical, but I'll try my best to elucidate.

Do note: All the data used in this article is freely available in the public domain, and open to scrutiny.

While going through the list of 'Most active users' for #ModiInQatar, a few accounts that popped up were of escort services!

Escort services? Interesting.

We decided we should look at the 'heatmap' to find where these tweets were originating from, but didn't find much.

Yes, there were quite a few tweets from the UAE.

It intrigued us enough and we decided to look up other hashtags that were trending. The first one was #UdtaKejriFundsUdtaPunjab.

When I looked at the list of most active Twitter users, there was a striking similarity among many followers, apart from the fact that they were tweeting the same content.

All of them had few followers, some as few as four, with only a handful of them following 158 people, and had 1.2K related tweets.

In a nutshell, we figured, someone, or some organisation, had created around 150 users. They had got them to randomly follow few other users and posted 1.2k tweets in all.

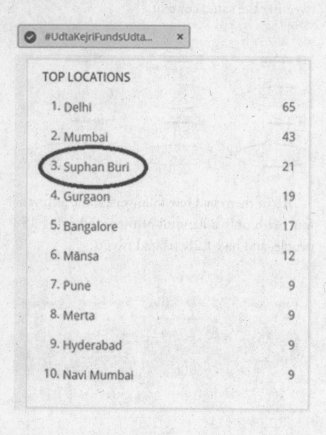

Interestingly, many of these users had Punjabi/ Sikh names. Because AAP is strongly contesting Punjab elections, and giving the Akali-BJP combine nightmares, I figured, someone was trying to build the 'perception' that the people of Punjab are tweeting against Arvind Kejriwal and AAP.

But here's when things appeared more interesting.

When I looked at the heatmap now, I found that many of the tweets were coming from Thailand out of all the places.

What were so many 'bhakts' doing on the beaches of Thailand?

I looked more closely at the location and found the users were tweeting from Suhan Buri, a state in central Thailand, which ranks third in the top locations.

At this point, Modiji was in the middle of touring Afghanistan, Qatar, Switzerland, USA and Mexico. I decided to track the hashtags around each of the visits to try and figure out what was going on.

When he was wrapping up his Switzerland visit, I began to analyse the hashtag #ModiInSwitzerland.

Here I found the top users were old BJP followers. I know some of them because they have been consistently abusing me now for the past few years. They have a decent following, but here again, the heatmap pointed to Thailand as a hotspot for the tweets.

This time, however, the location pointed to a new place, Phra Nakhon Si Ayutthaya, another state from central Thailand, that ranks fourth in the top locations. I had never heard of this place earlier and had to do a Google search to find out if it was even a place.

Then Modiji reached the US. First I looked at the hashtag, #ModiInUS. It did have some tweets from Thailand, but not a substantial number. Then I decided to look at the hashtag #ModiInUSA.

Appendix B

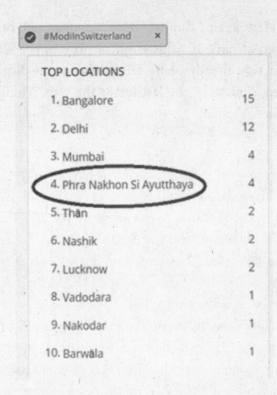

Here again "Suphan Buri" was featured, but down at rank 10. This is no surprise as the US visit was already being talked about and didn't need a push. In the last leg of the visit, Modiji visited Mexico.

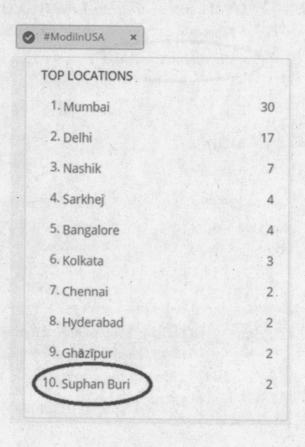

This day the hashtag #ModiInMexico was trending, and after the visit was culminated, I analysed the data. Again, Thailand was featured prominently on the heatmap.

Suphan Buri, the same nondescript state in central Thailand, was again at the fourth spot in the list of top locations tweeting about the issue.

For me, the question was, are the Thais really interested in PM Modi or is there an Indian population there, which loves Modi only too much?

A bit of research suggested that neither of the two is true.

The most talked about issue in this duration in Thailand on Twitter was the surgery of their ageing king and neither of the two states has a sizeable Indian population.

So what is it?

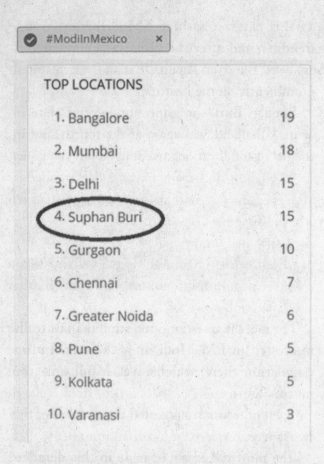

| #ModiInMexico | × |

TOP LOCATIONS

1. Bangalore	19
2. Mumbai	18
3. Delhi	15
4. Suphan Buri	15
5. Gurgaon	10
6. Chennai	7
7. Greater Noida	6
8. Pune	5
9. Kolkata	5
10. Varanasi	3

I began to wait till the BJP trended a seemingly neutral hashtag with no global interest. Soon, #TransformingIndia began to trend.

Well, how do I know that the BJP trended it? Well because no less than the prime minister used this hashtag for his account.

I switched on my analytics.

The heatmap again showed Thailand was a prominent location for most of the tweets that were emerging.

This one is far more interesting than the other hashtags I had analysed before. Here, the prime minister's official account @PMOIndia, as well as his ministerial colleagues Smriti Irani, Rajnath Singh and Manohar Parrikar were tweeting too.

I tried to explore the locations from where these tweets were happening. As expected, 'Suphan Buri' was among the top locations, proudly placed at number 3. 'Phra Nakhon Si Ayutthaya' was at number 9.

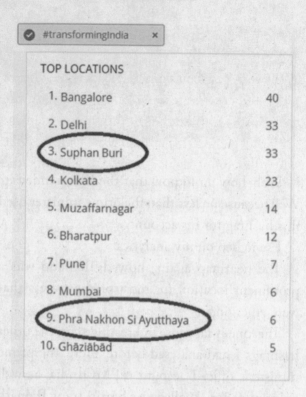

So, what does all this mean? Can't there be actual supporters who might be tweeting for Modiji and BJP?

Well, quite possibly, there would be a few, but the volume that makes these places show up regularly on the list of top locations is not that easy to gather with a few sporadic followers.

There are only two possible explanations:

a) The easier explanation: BJP leaders or some of their supporters are using VPN (Virtual Private Network) to hide their location and identity. Hiding behind this wall, they are creating fake handles on a regular basis and helping the BJP hashtags. This explains the usage of the same content from multiple handles, as in the case of #UdtaKejriFundsUdtaPunjab. This also means that their actual supporters have gone silent.

b) The darker explanation: BJP has hired some marketing agency in Thailand to do their dirty work. This includes creating fake users, abusing leaders of other parties and creating a negative perception against leaders like Arvind Kejriwal.

If the latter is the case, then the situation is much more alarming and it means that BJP has recognised that its support base online is depleting, and they have now gone into damage control mode.

One thing which is amply clear is that BJP has some explaining to do. I urge IT minister

Ravishankar Prasad to look into this. May be he could shed some light on whether this too is part of the #DigitalIndia initiative?

Suggested Reading

'JNU videos doctored: Forensic report; Smriti Irani's aide Shilpi Tewari under lens'

http://economictimes.indiatimes.com/news/ politics-and-nation/jnu-videos-doctored-forensic-report-smriti-iranis-aide-shilpi-tewari-under-lens/articleshow/51232360.cms

'Shilpi Tiwari, Irani's close aide is the latest to face the JNU heat'

http://www.hindustantimes.com/india/shilpi-tiwari-smriti-irani-s-close-aide-is-the -latest-victim-in-jnu-row/story-mFS9jFnNiHodeh9 hcQaSMI.html

'JNU: Forensic lab finds Kanhaiya videos doctored, Irani's aide faces heat online'

http://www.thenewsminute.com/article/jnu-forensic-lab-finds-kanhaiya-videos-doctored-iranis-aide-faces-heat-online-39661

Acknowledgements

This is the biggest investigation I have done in my career. It has taken me two years and countless interviews. None of it would have been possible without the following:

Ram Madhav, who gave me an extensive taped interview and spoke with deep knowledge and insight about the broader perspective of the RSS and BJP's social media agenda.

Arun Shourie, who is always unfailingly generous and who shared his sharp insight, speaking at length on tape about his experience.

Former chief election commissioner S.Y. Quraishi, who was patient and explained at great length how he wanted to stop incitement on social media as a political ploy.

Former MP and one-time editor of the *Indian Express*, *Hindustan Times* and *Times of India*, H.K.

Dua, who shared his valuable insights into how the RSS works.

Ankit Lal, who gave me an insight into AAP and the big fight with the BJP on social media; and IT engineer Siddharth Bhaskar, who corroborated his study.

Abhisar Sharma, who bravely spoke out in an email interview.

Dilip Cherian, who spoke up when most people in PR would have maintained a judicious silence.

Senior officials with the Ministry of Home Affairs, Intelligence Bureau, Department of Telecom, Ministry of Communications and IT, Ministry of Information and Broadcasting and Ministry of Finance who gave me insider accounts of what was going on in the social media space in the government, as well as some vital documents and leads to follow.

The BJP and RSS leaders who went out of the way to help me get a toehold in the world of trolls, making introductions and helping me set up meetings.

My trolls, thank you for meeting me and agreeing to talk. I promised you anonymity and I intend to stick to my word.

Acknowledgements

Finally, thanks to Sadhavi Khosla, whose courage and generosity has not just been an inspiration but was central to this investigation. Most of us take wrong turns in our lives; few have the strength to try to set things right.

A Note on the Author

Swati Chaturvedi is a journalist. This is her second book.

juggernaut

THE APP FOR INDIAN READERS

Fresh, original books tailored for mobile and for India. Starting at ₹10.

juggernaut.in

CRAFTED FOR MOBILE READING

Thought you would never read a book on mobile? Let us prove you wrong.

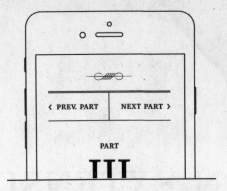

Beautiful Typography

The quality of print transferred
to your mobile. Forget ugly PDFs.

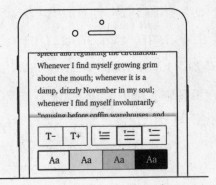

Customizable Reading

Read in the font size, spacing
and background of your liking.

AN EXTENSIVE LIBRARY

Including fresh, new, original Juggernaut books from the likes of Sunny Leone, Praveen Swami, Husain Haqqani, Umera Ahmed, Rujuta Diwekar and lots more. Plus, books from partner publishers and loads of free classics. Whichever genre you like, there's a book waiting for you.

DON'T JUST READ; INTERACT

We're changing the reading experience from passive to active.

Ask authors questions

Get all your answers from the horse's mouth.
Juggernaut authors actually reply to every
question they can.

Rate and review

Let everyone know of your favourite reads or
critique the finer points of a book – you will be
heard in a community of like-minded readers.

Gift books to friends

For a book-lover, there's no nicer gift than
a book personally picked. You can even
do it anonymously if you like.

Enjoy new book formats

Discover serials released in parts over
time, picture books including comics,
and story-bundles at discounted rates.
And coming soon, audiobooks.

4

LOWEST PRICES & ONE-TAP BUYING

Books start at ₹10 with regular discounts and free previews.

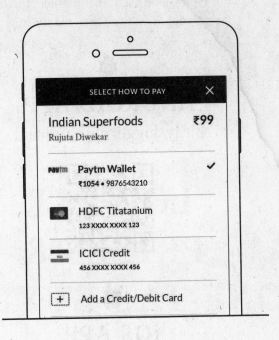

Paytm Wallet, Cards & Apple Payments

On Android, just add a Paytm Wallet once and buy any book with one tap. On iOS, pay with one tap with your iTunes-linked debit/credit card.

Click the QR Code with a QR scanner app
or type the link into the Internet browser
on your phone to download the app.

ANDROID APP

bit.ly/juggernautandroid

iOS APP

bit.ly/juggernautios

For our complete catalogue, visit www.juggernaut.in
To submit your book, send a synopsis and two
sample chapters to books@juggernaut.in
For all other queries, write to contact@juggernaut.in